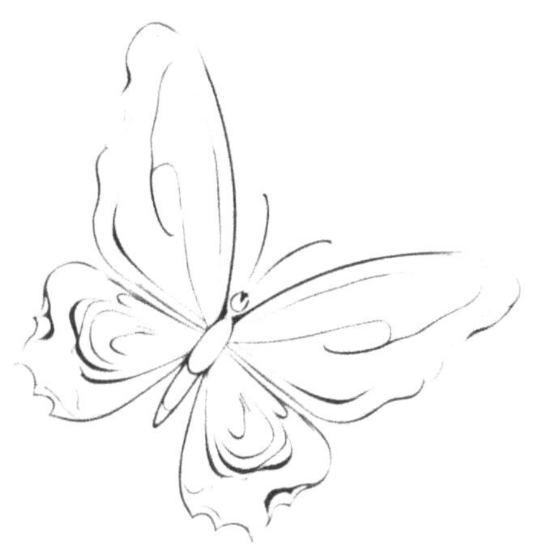
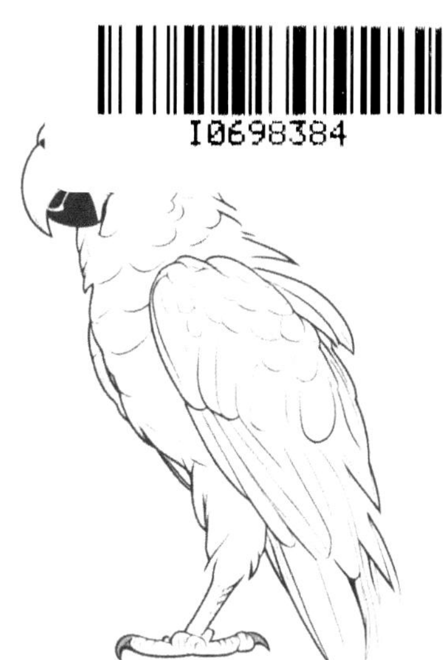

This Book Belongs to:

____

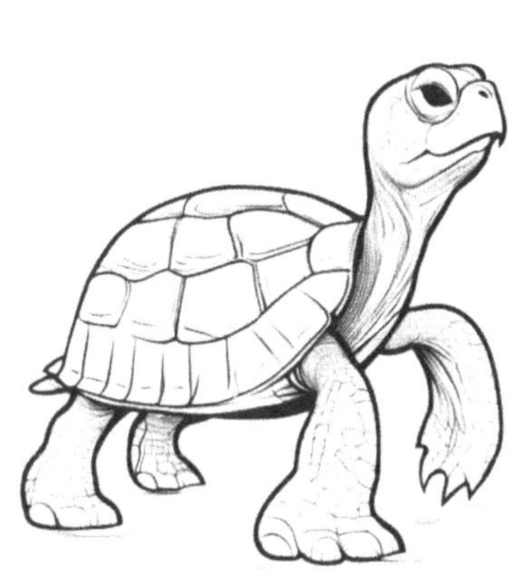
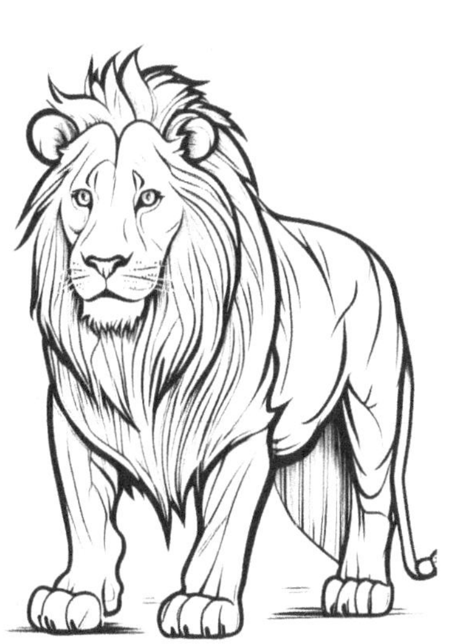

Test Color Page

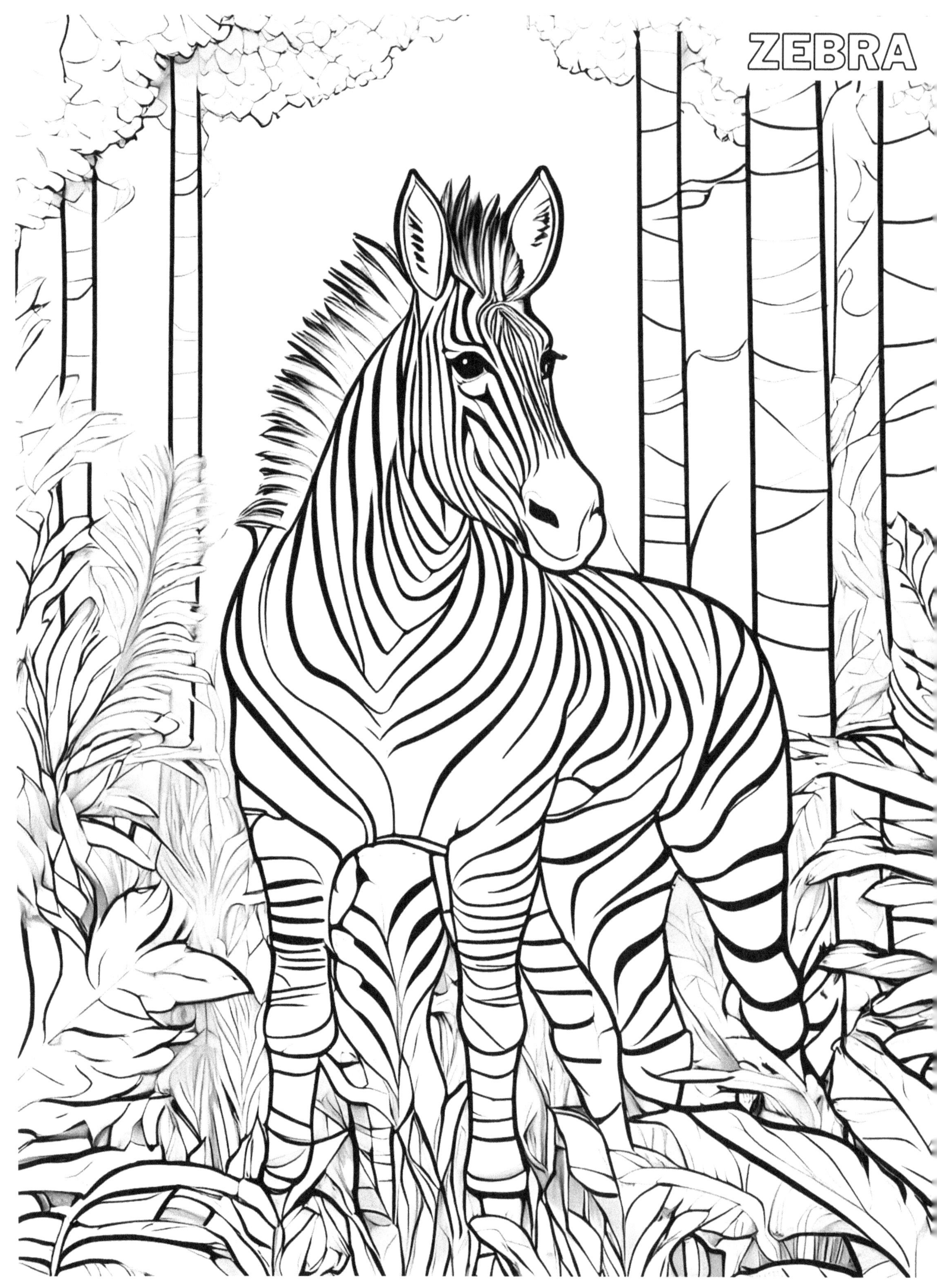
ZEBRA

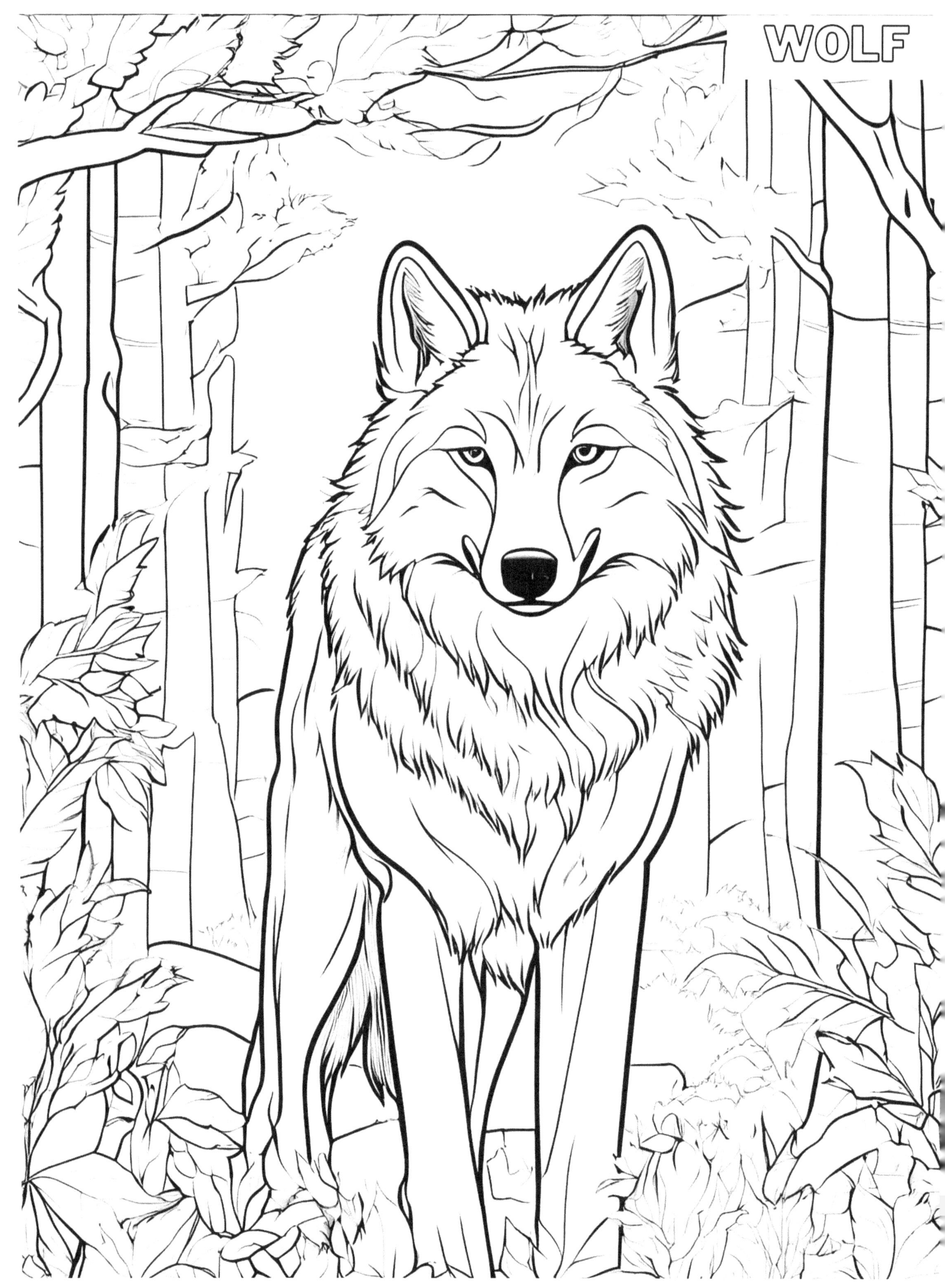
WOLF

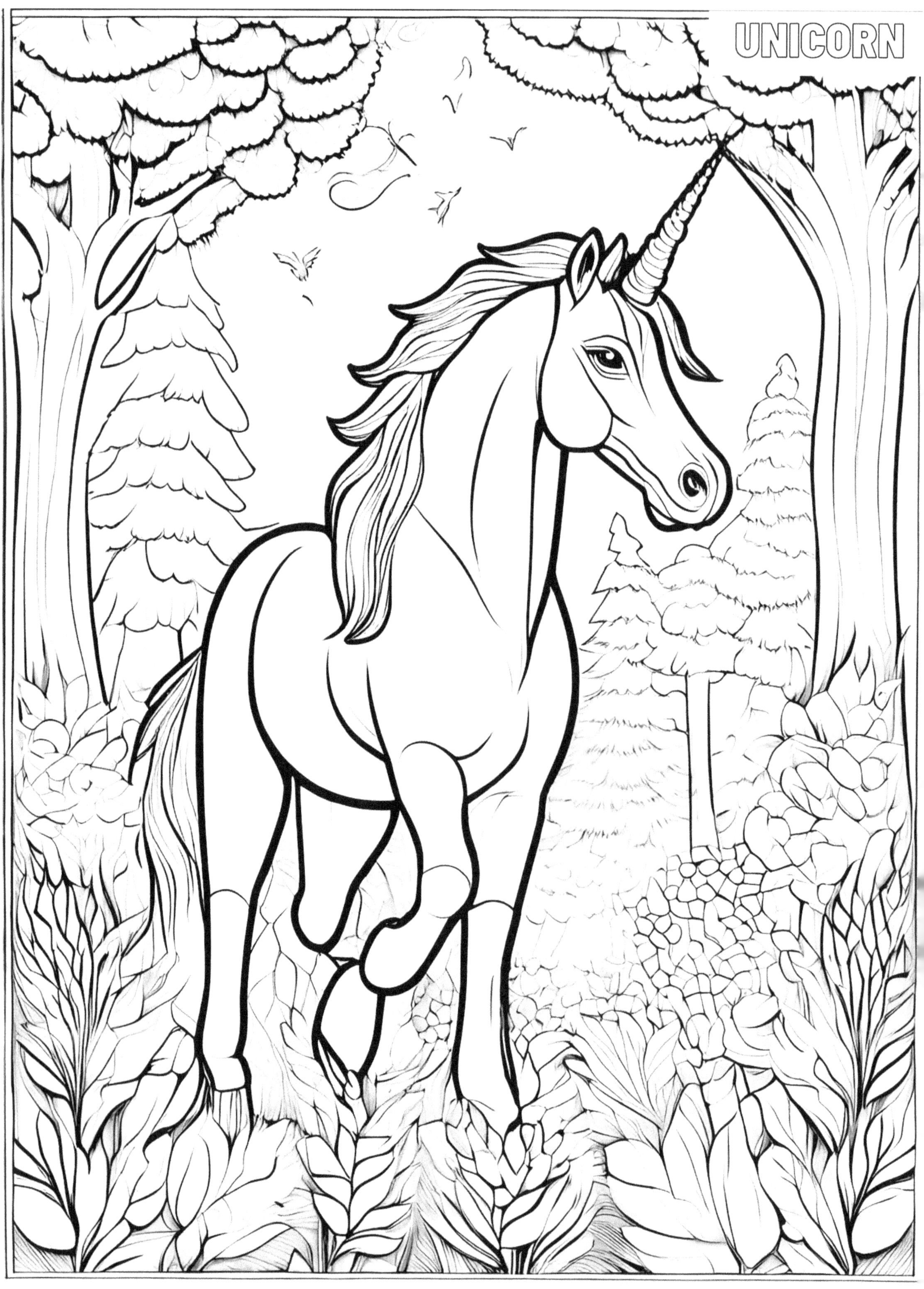
UNICORN

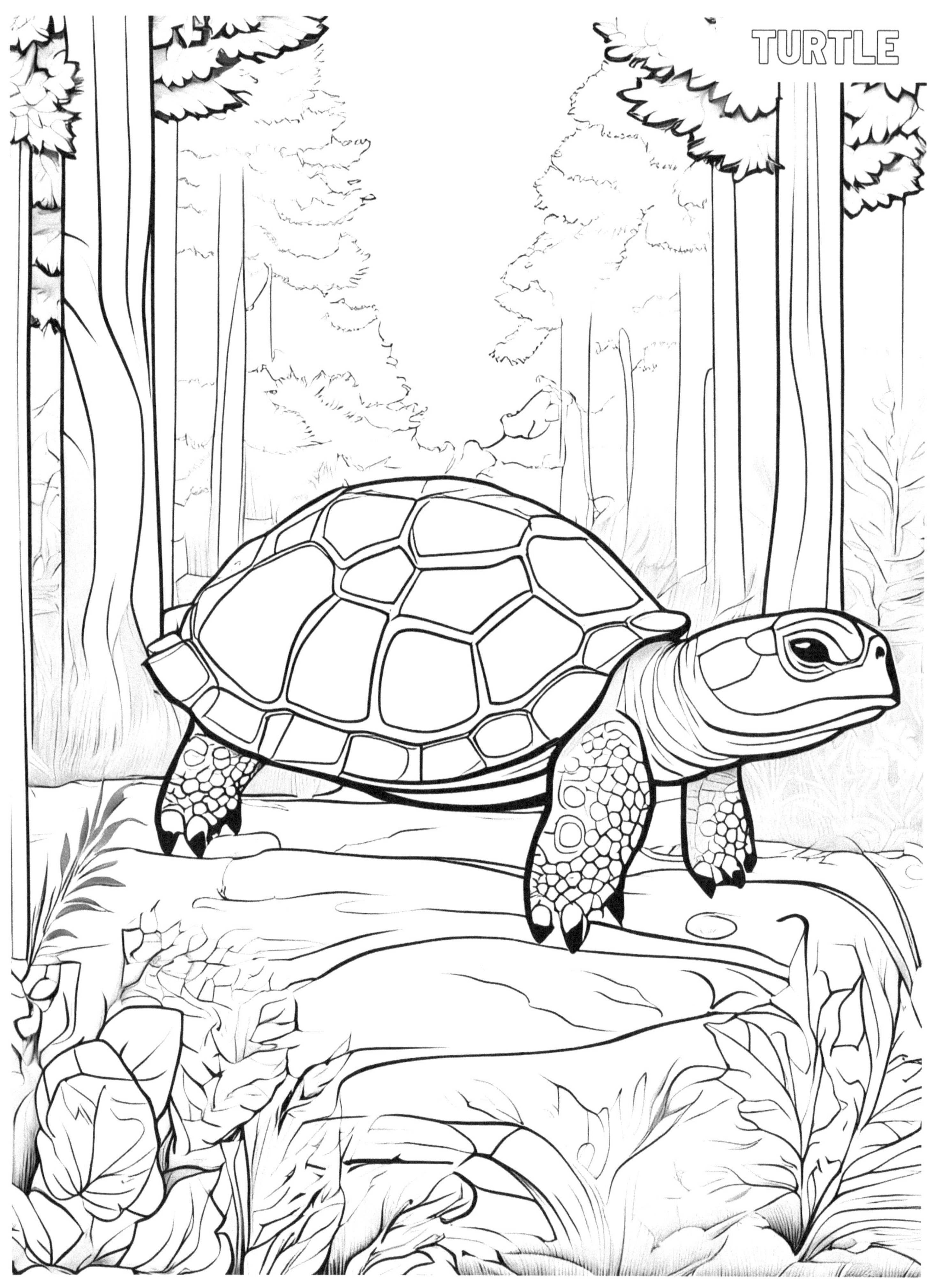
TURTLE

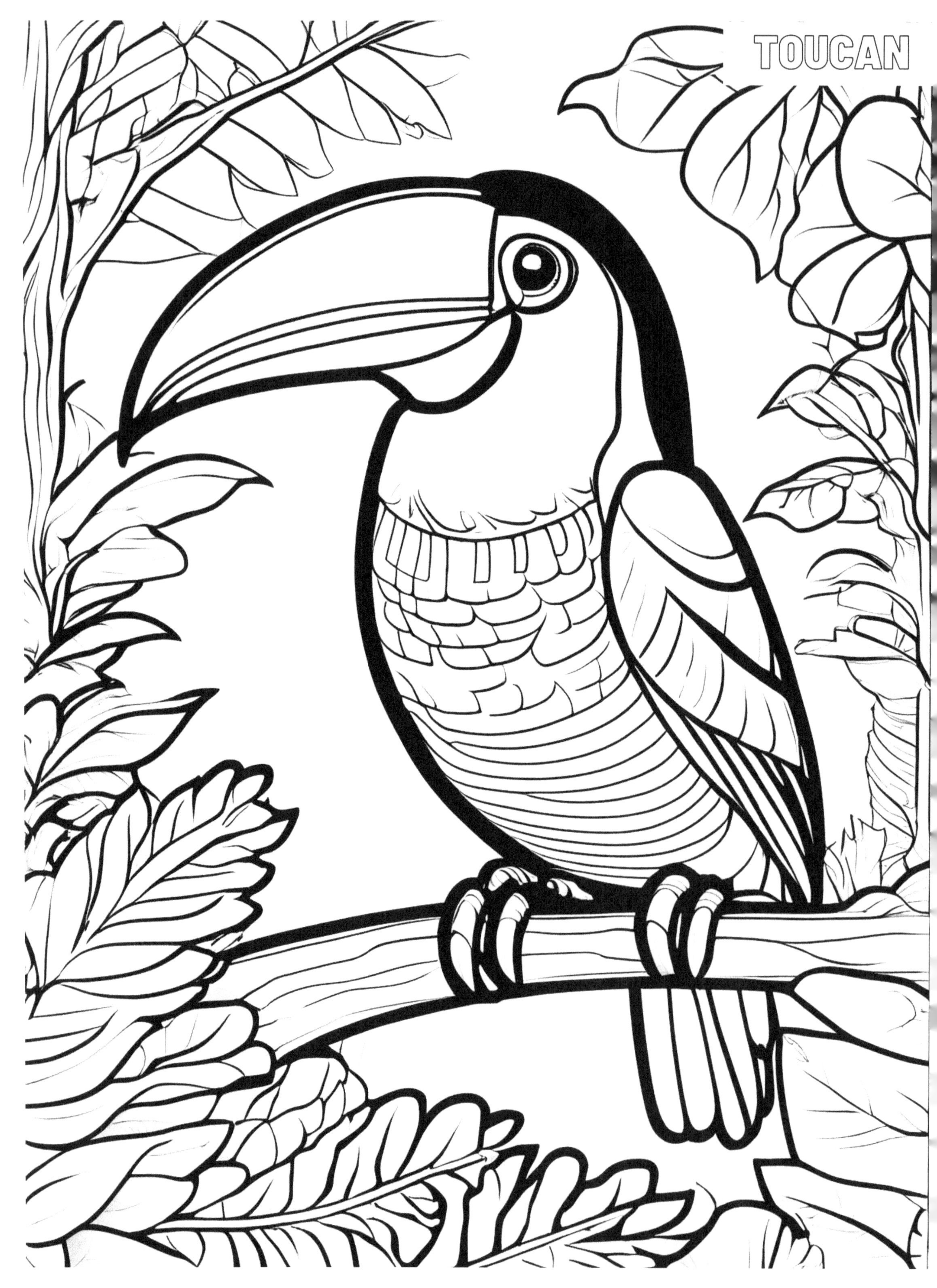
TOUCAN

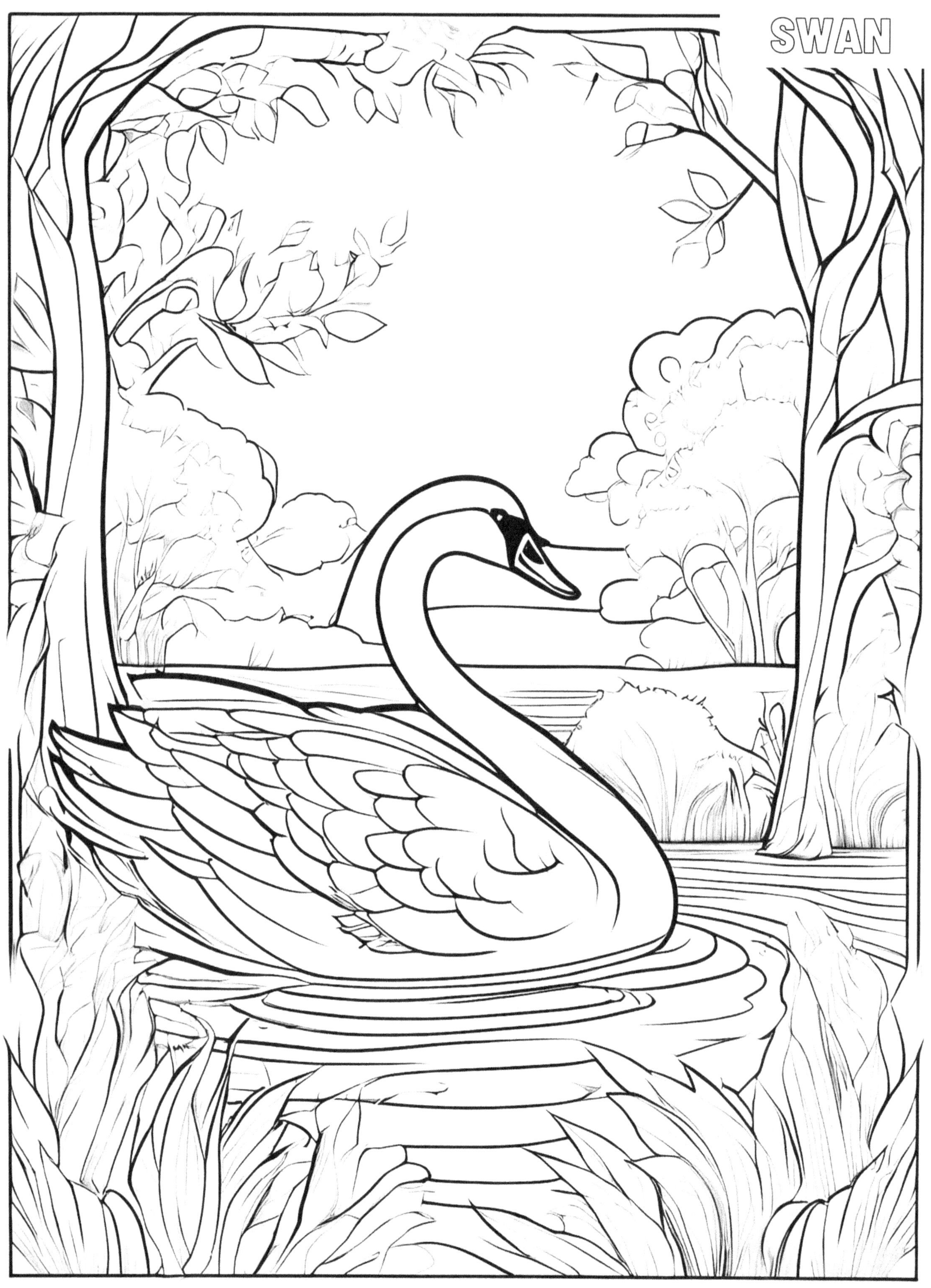
SWAN

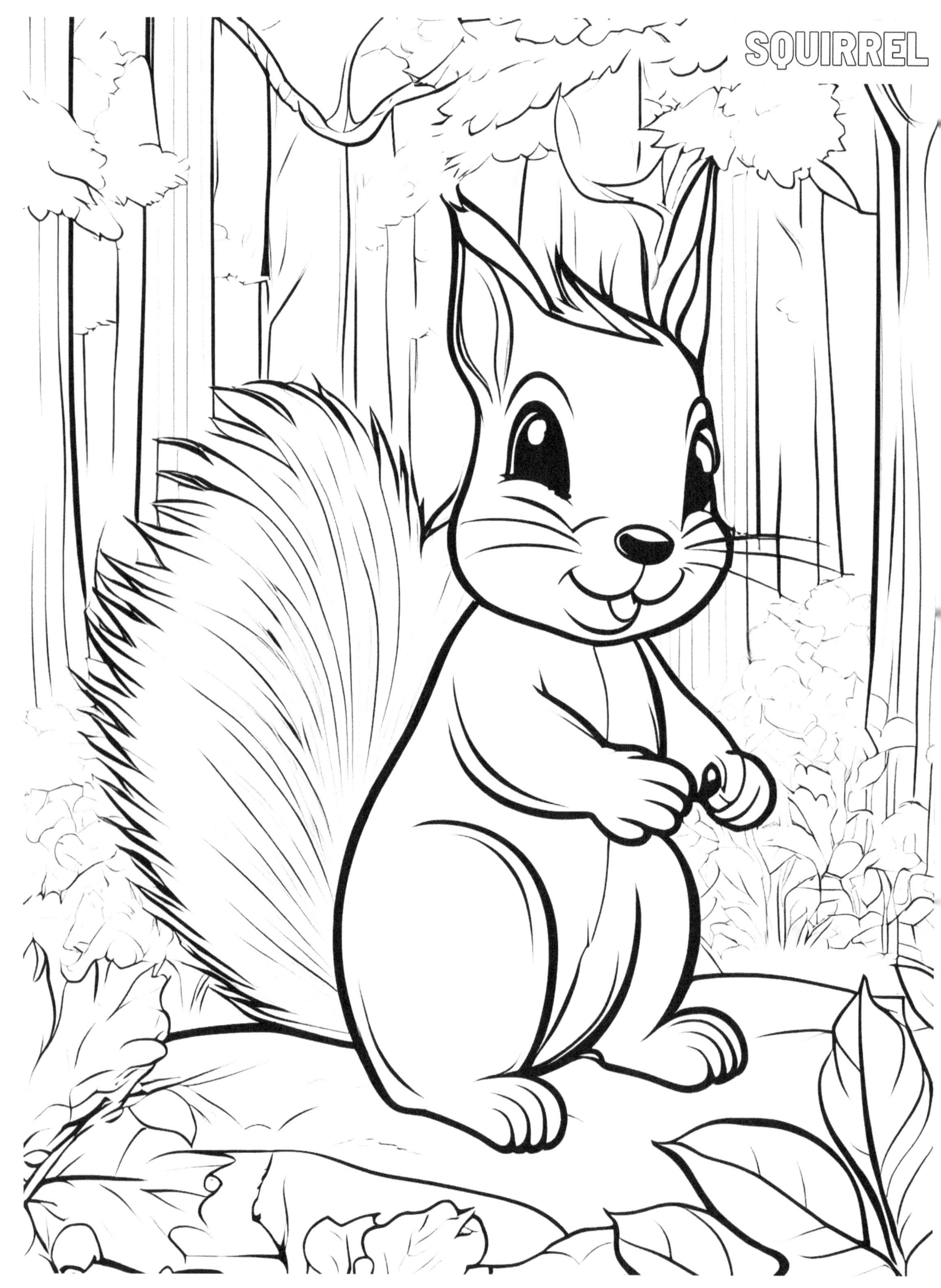

SQUIRREL

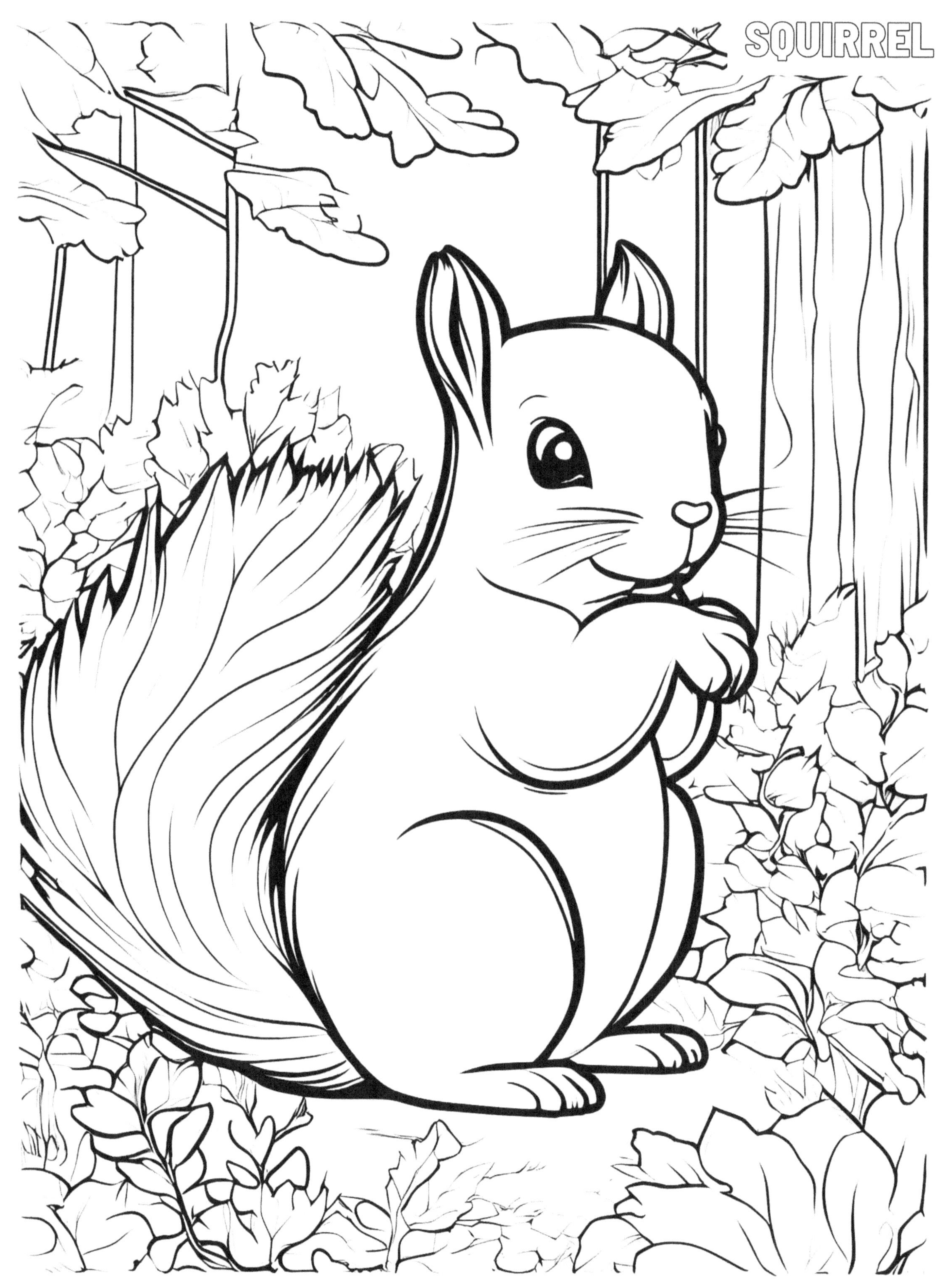

SQUIRREL

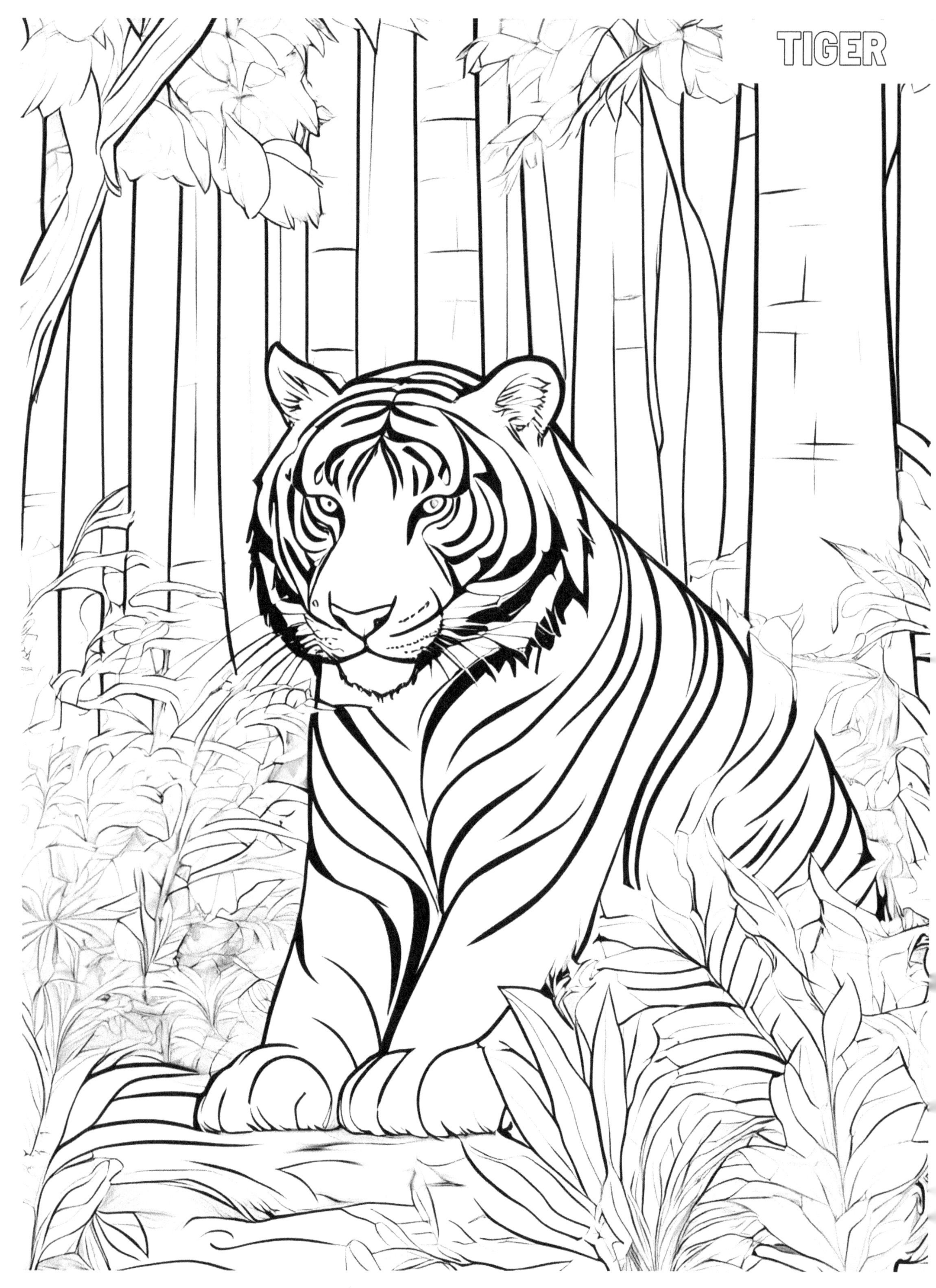
TIGER

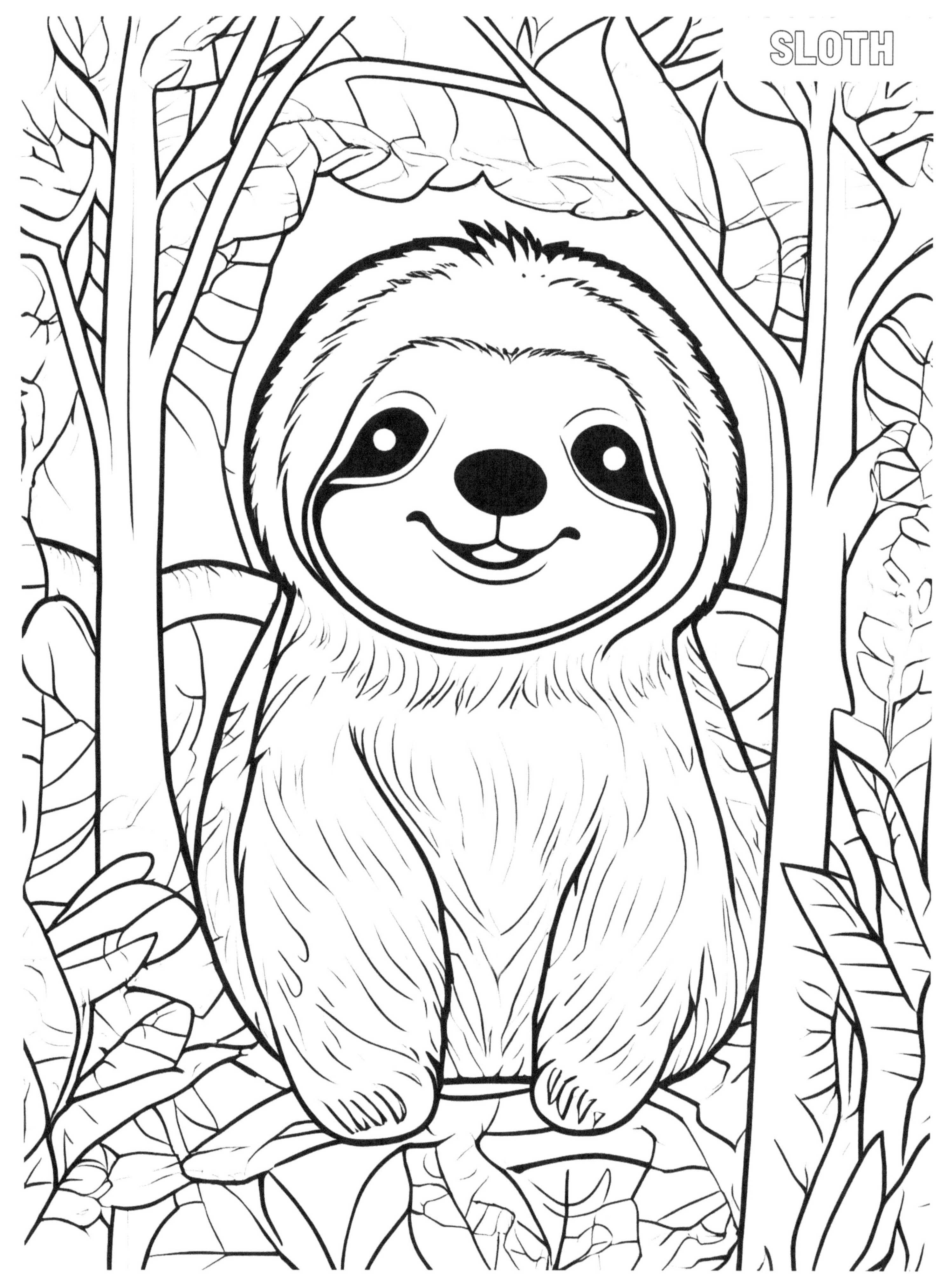

SLOTH

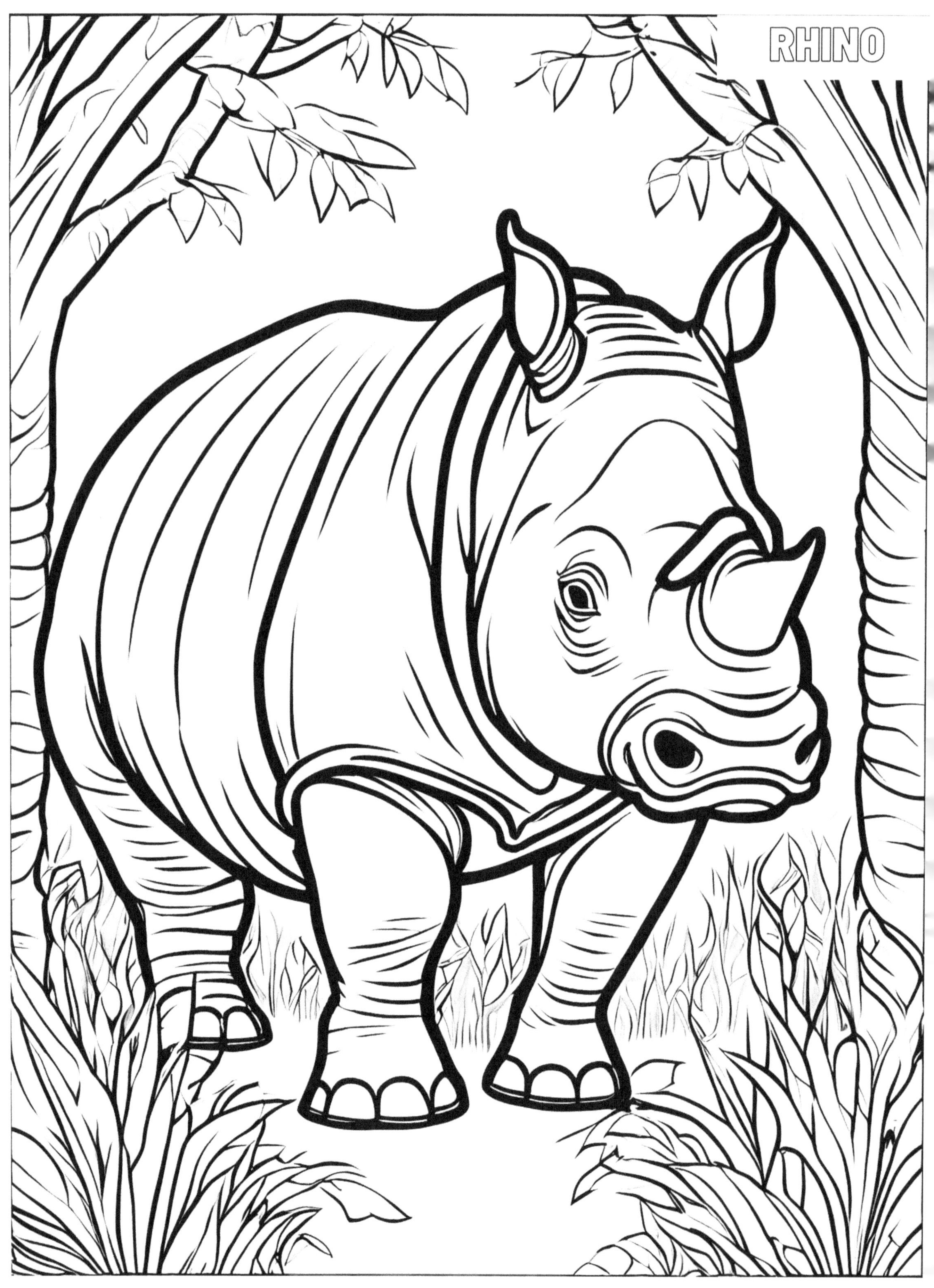
RHINO

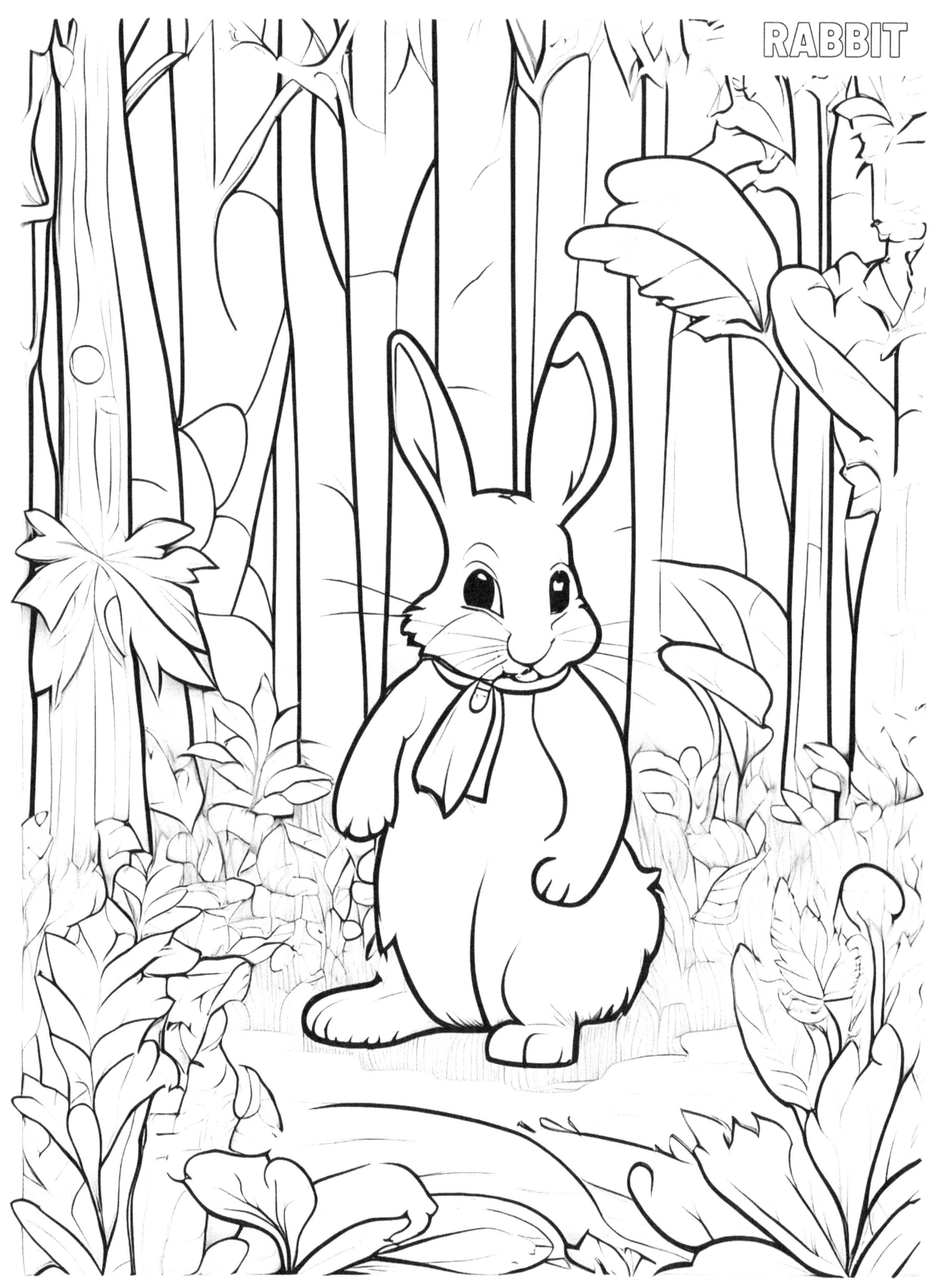
RABBIT

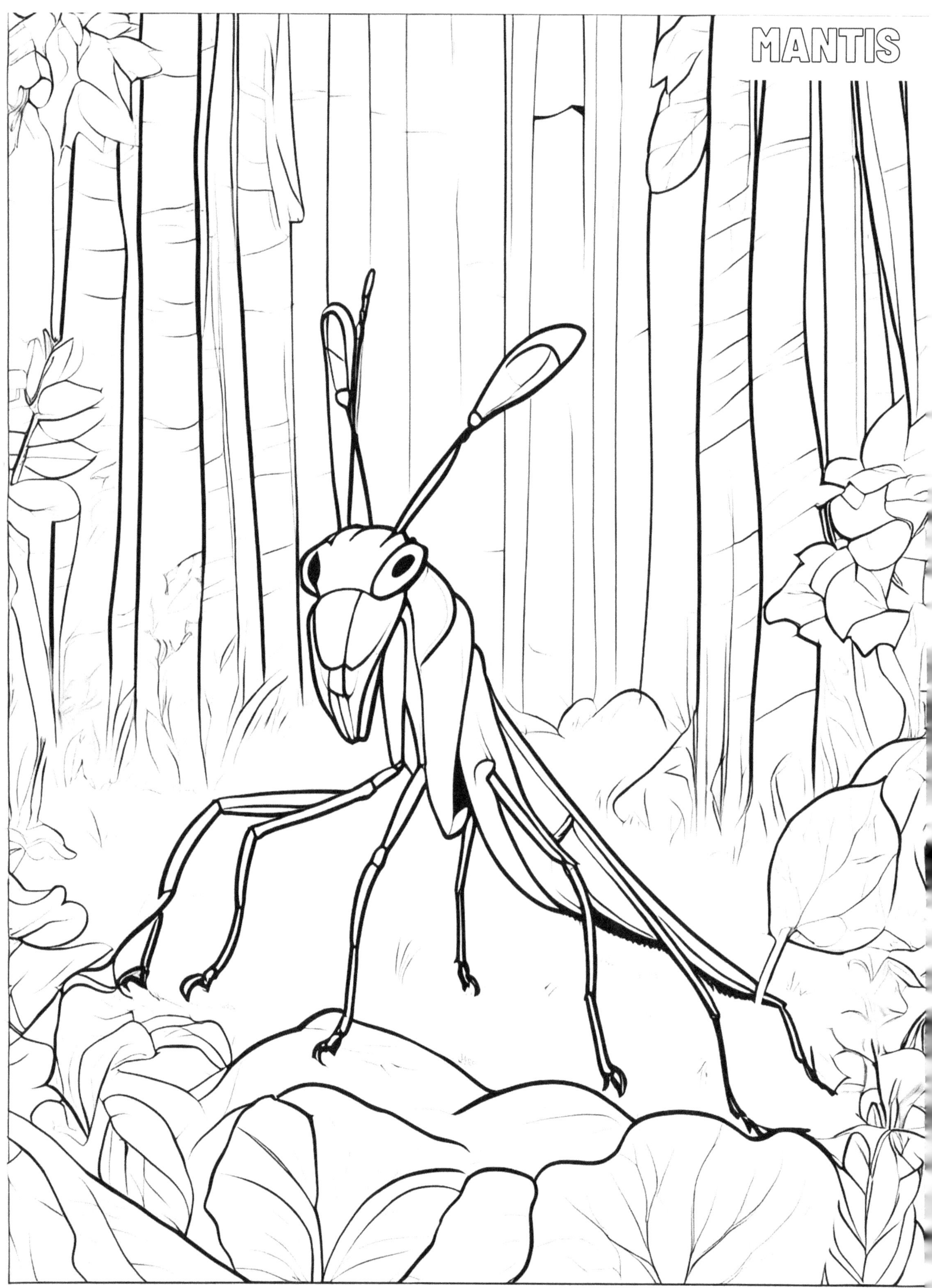
MANTIS

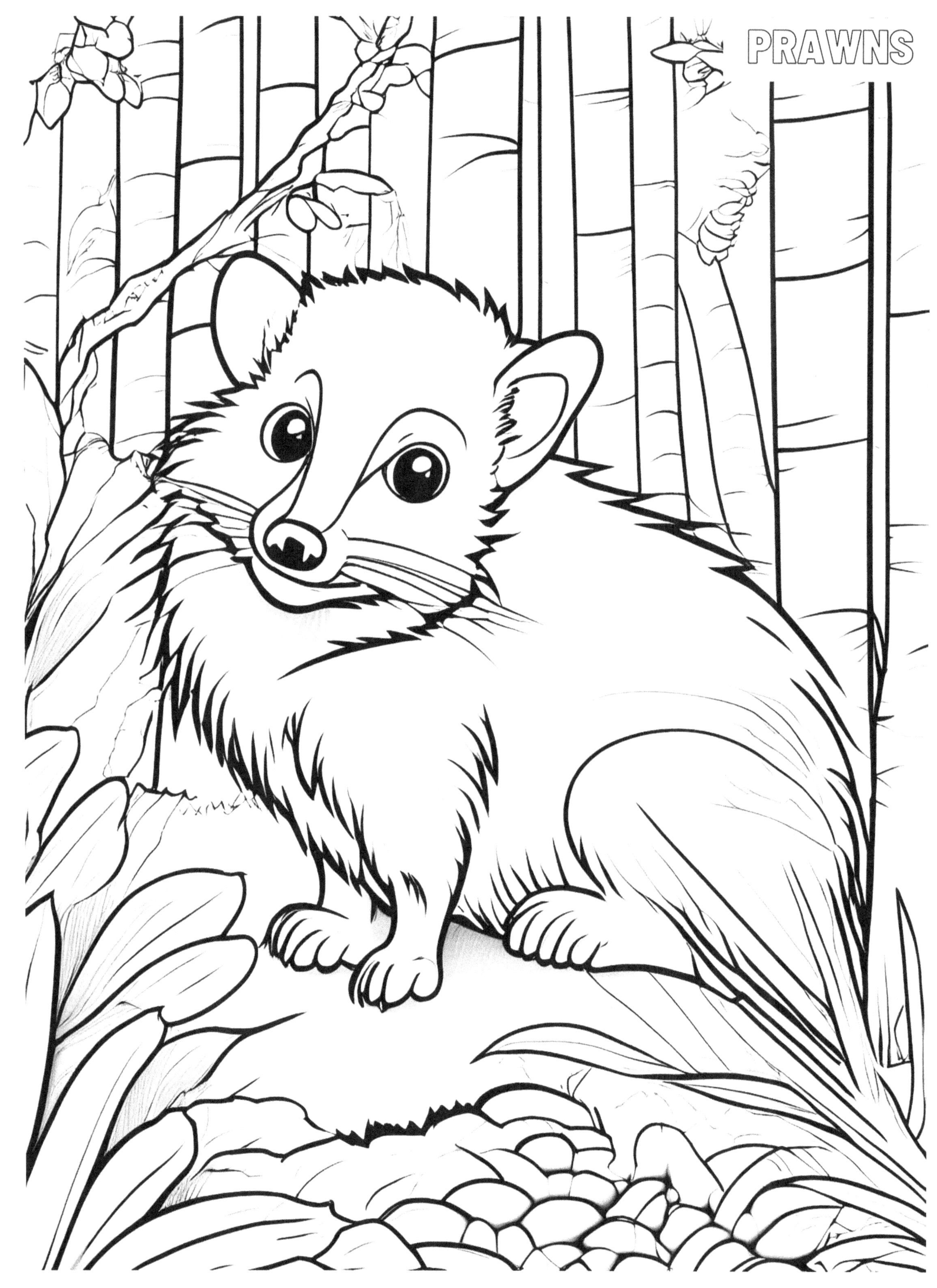
PRAWNS

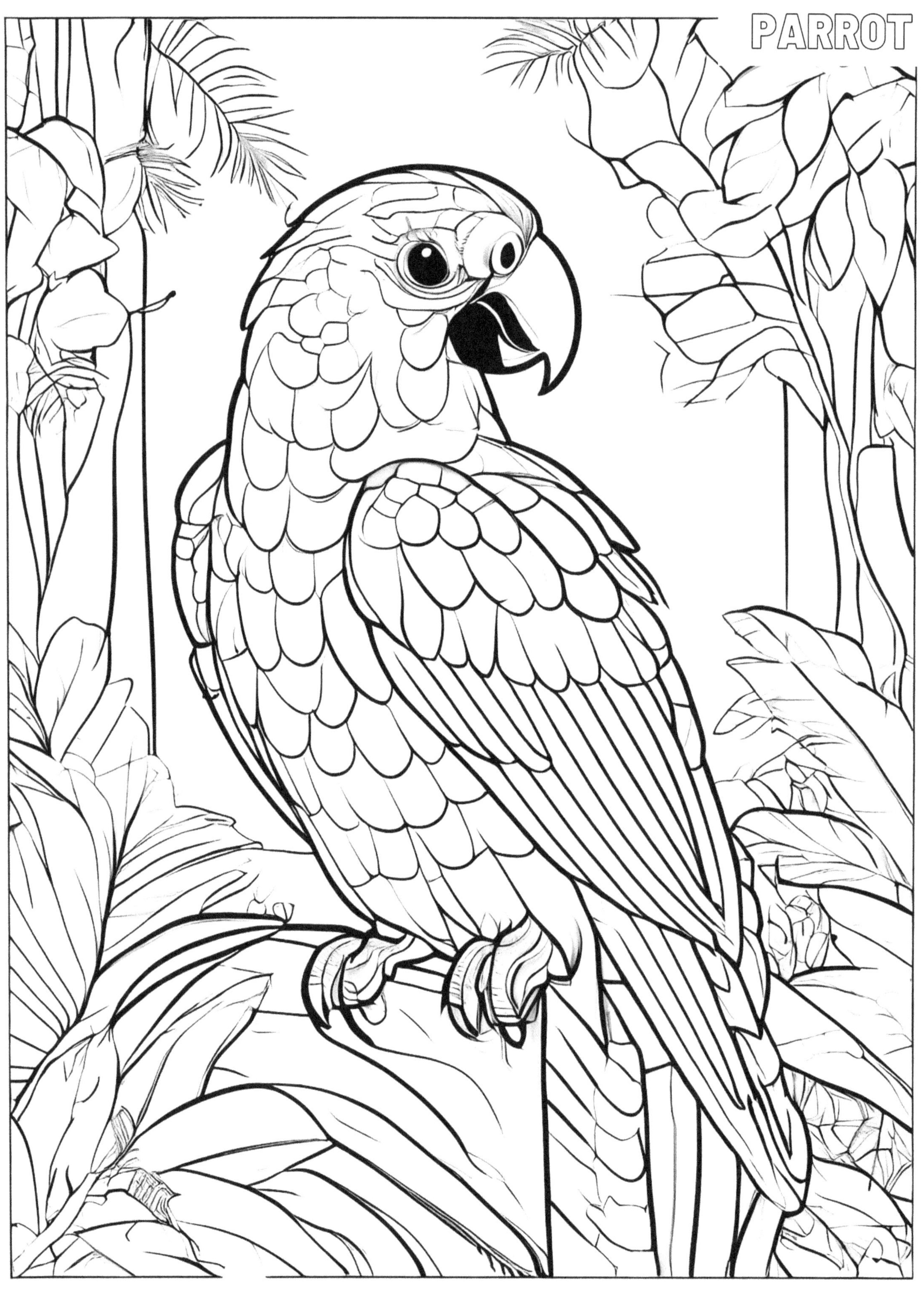
PARROT

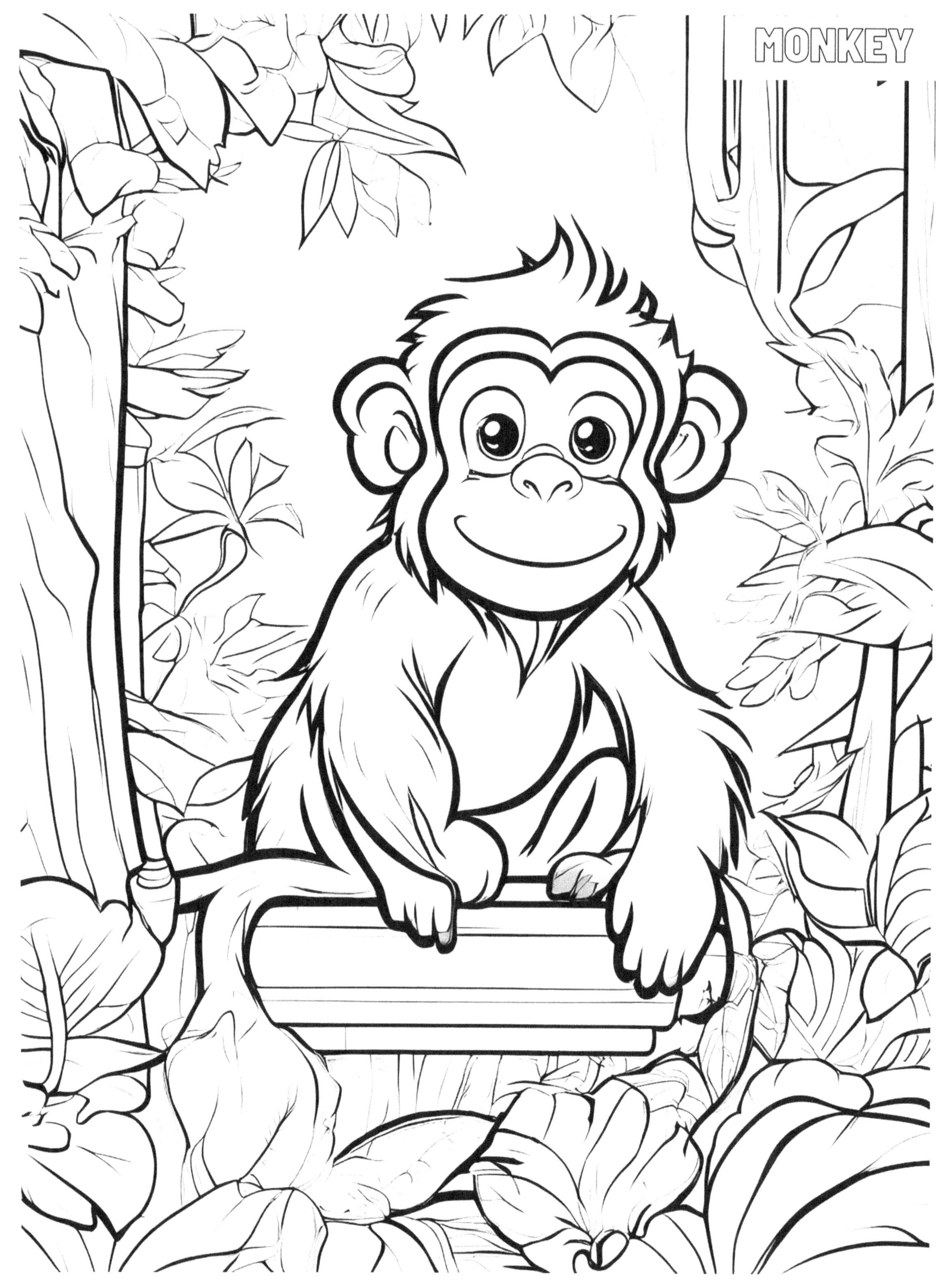
MONKEY

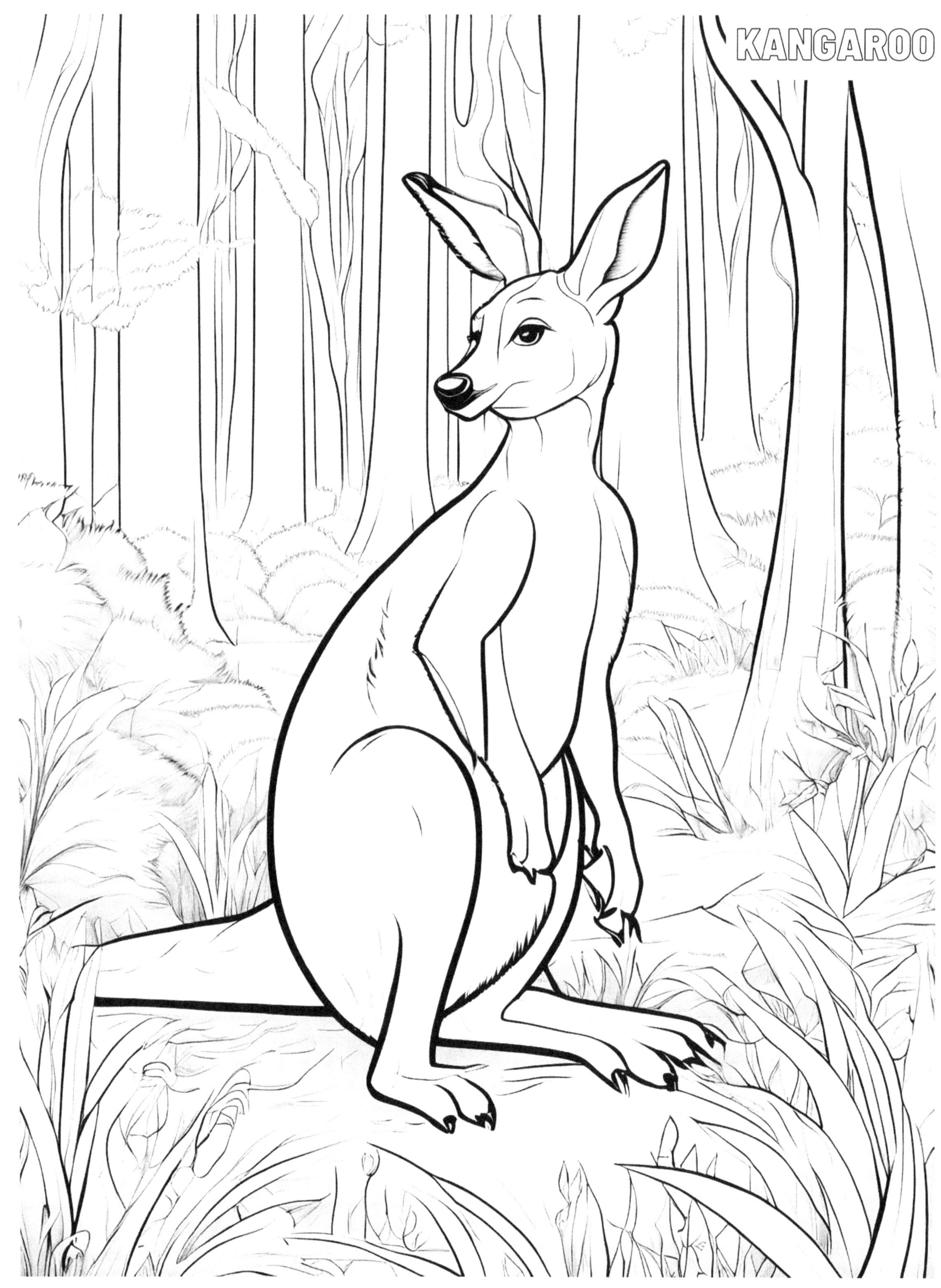
KANGAROO

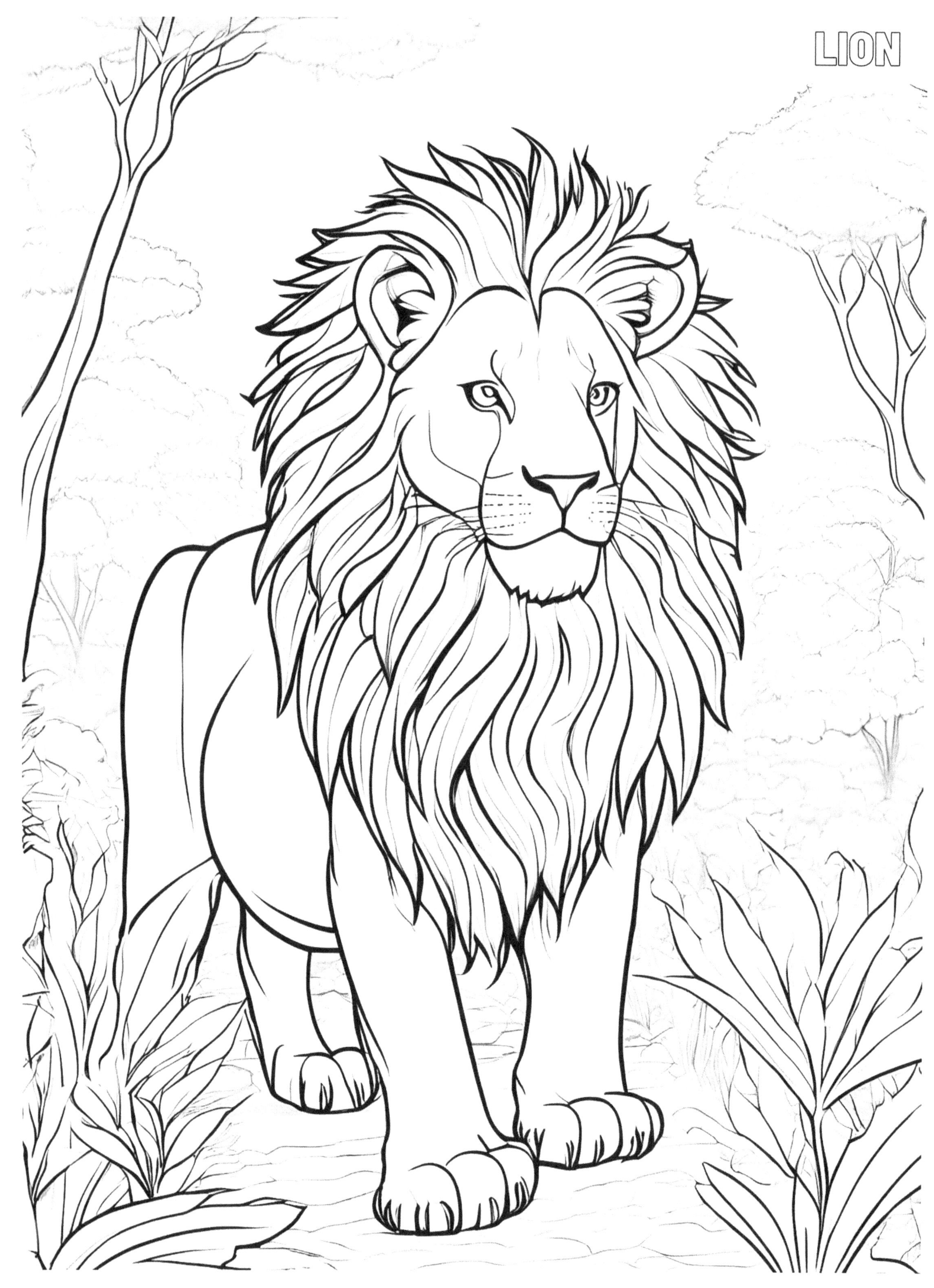
LION

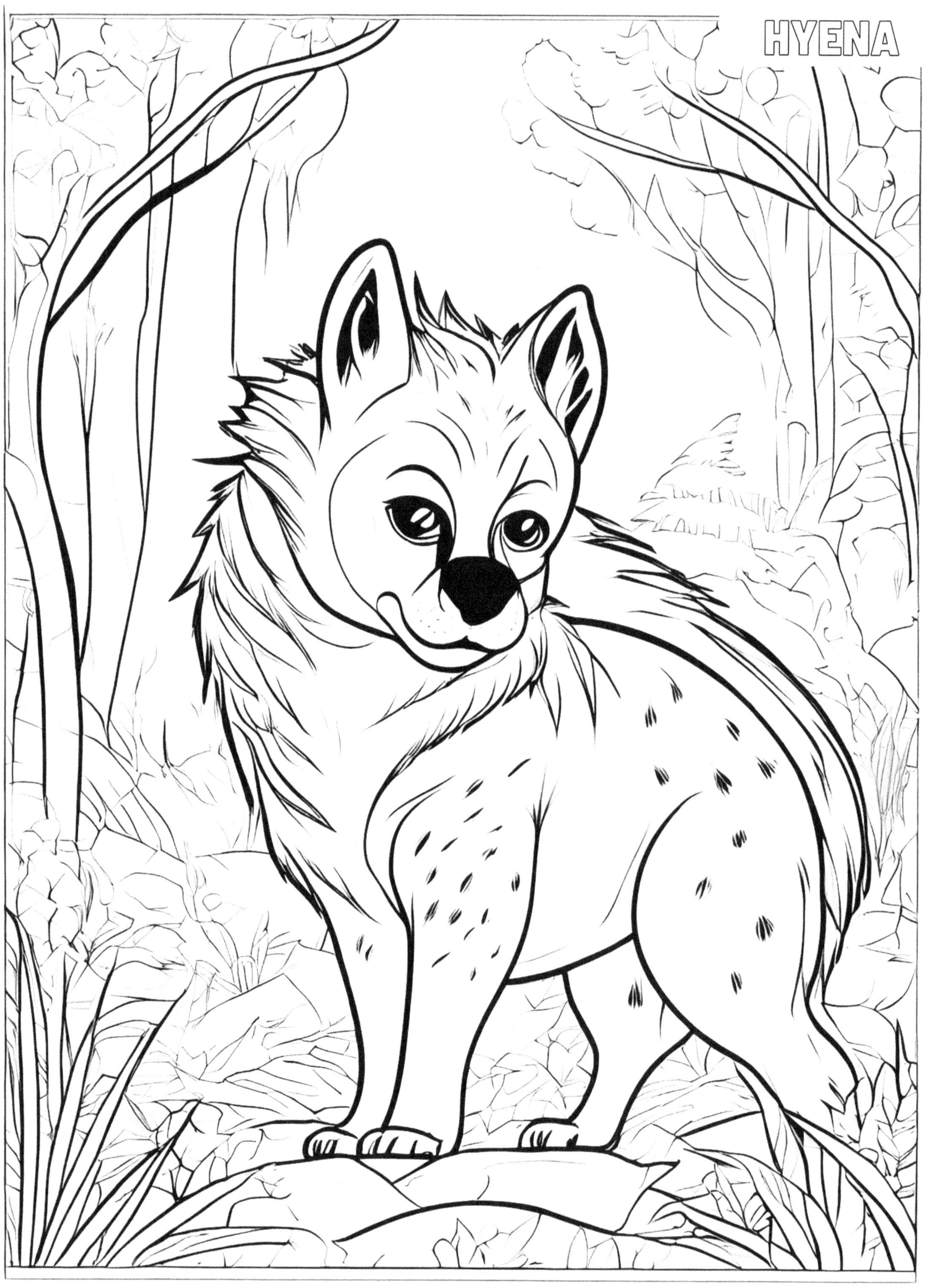
HYENA

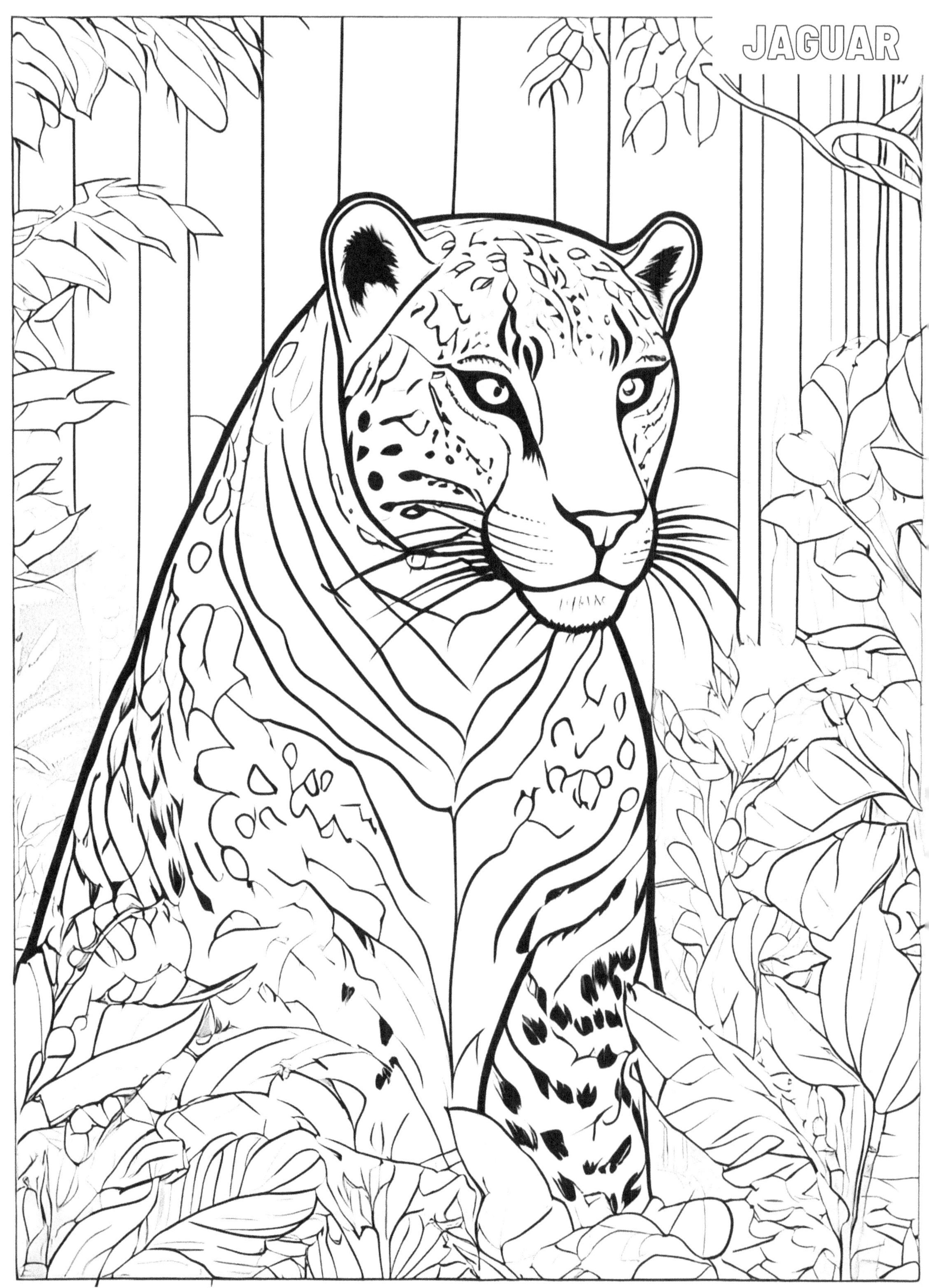
JAGUAR

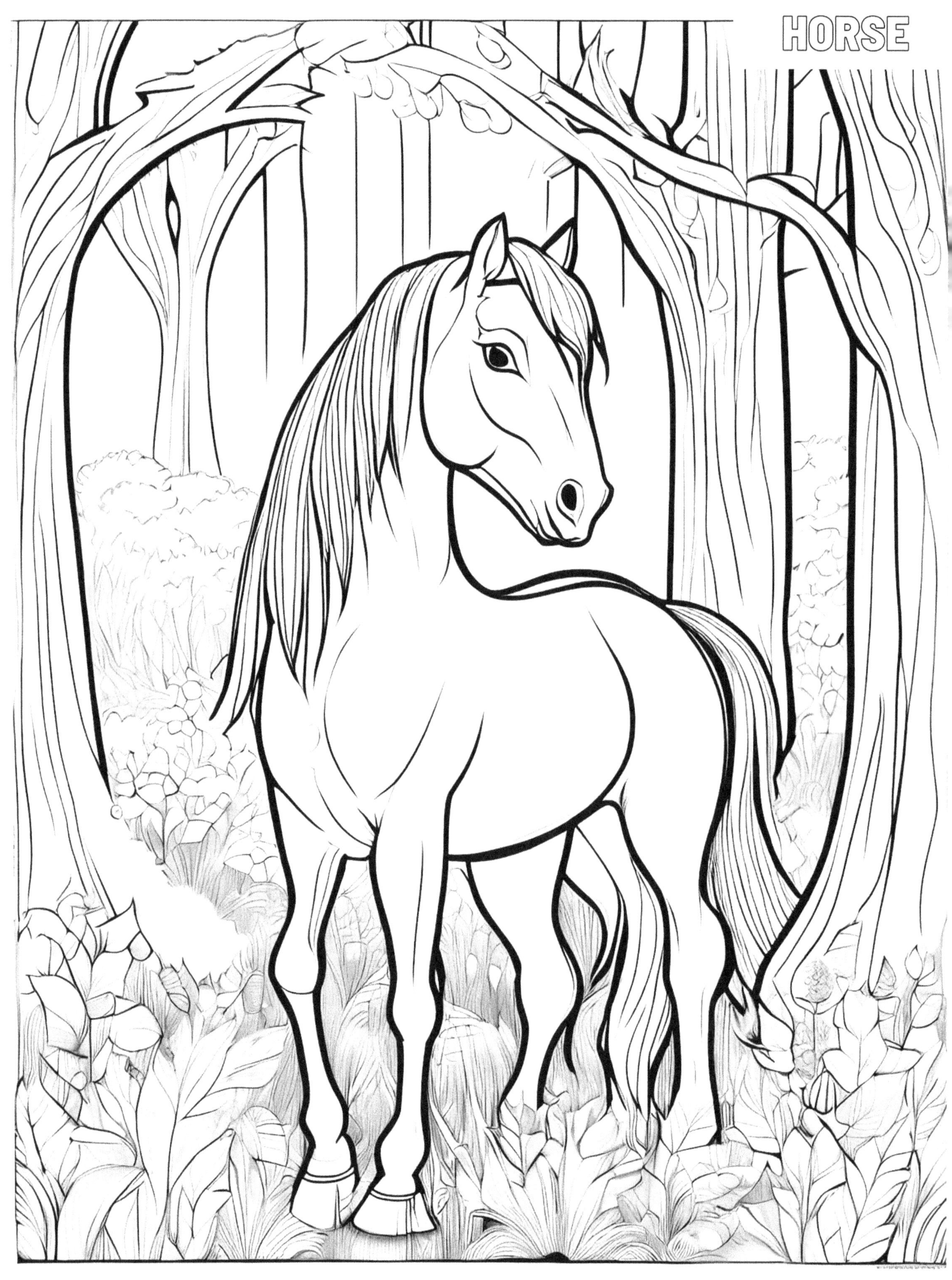
HORSE

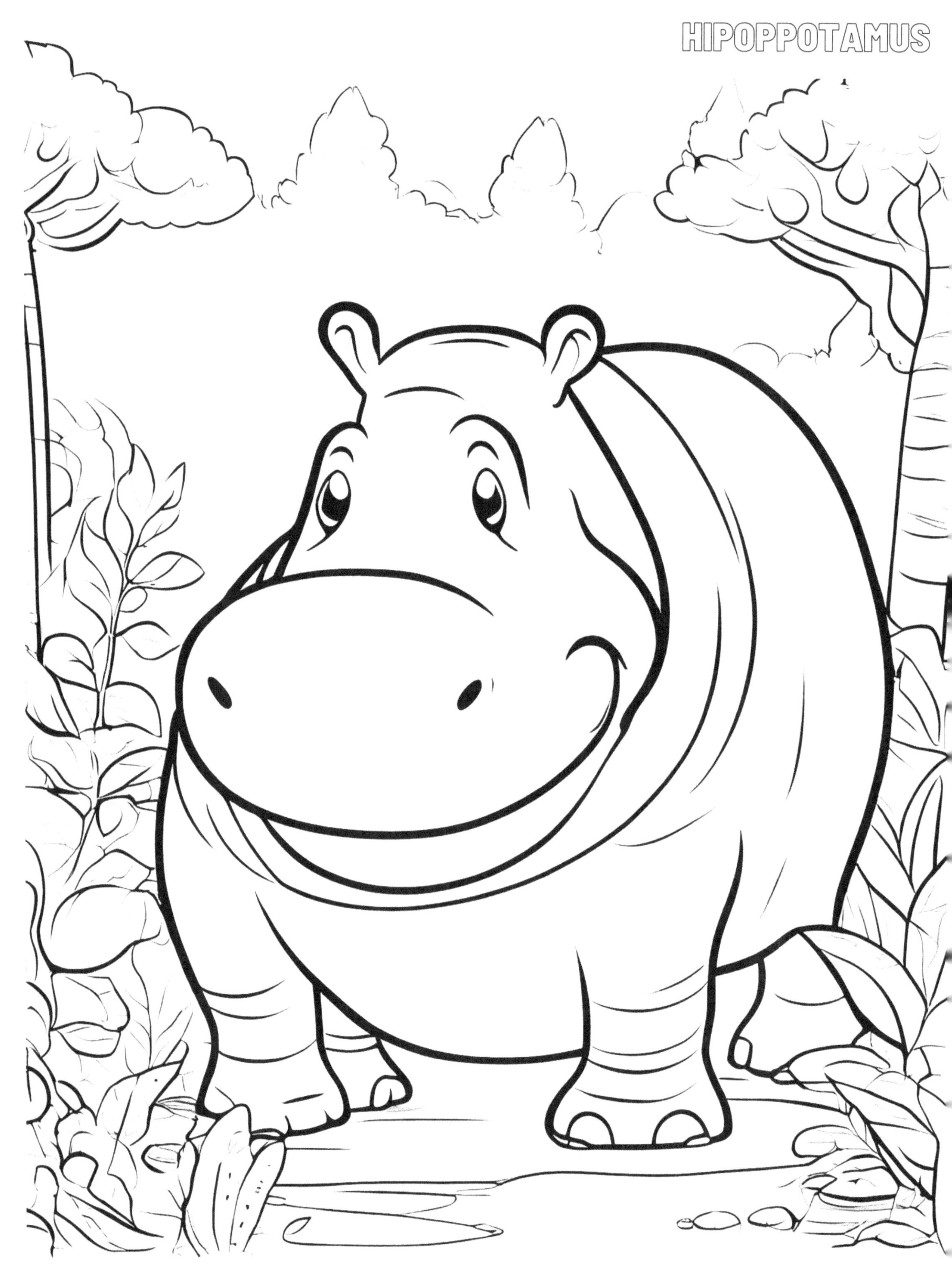
HIPOPPOTAMUS

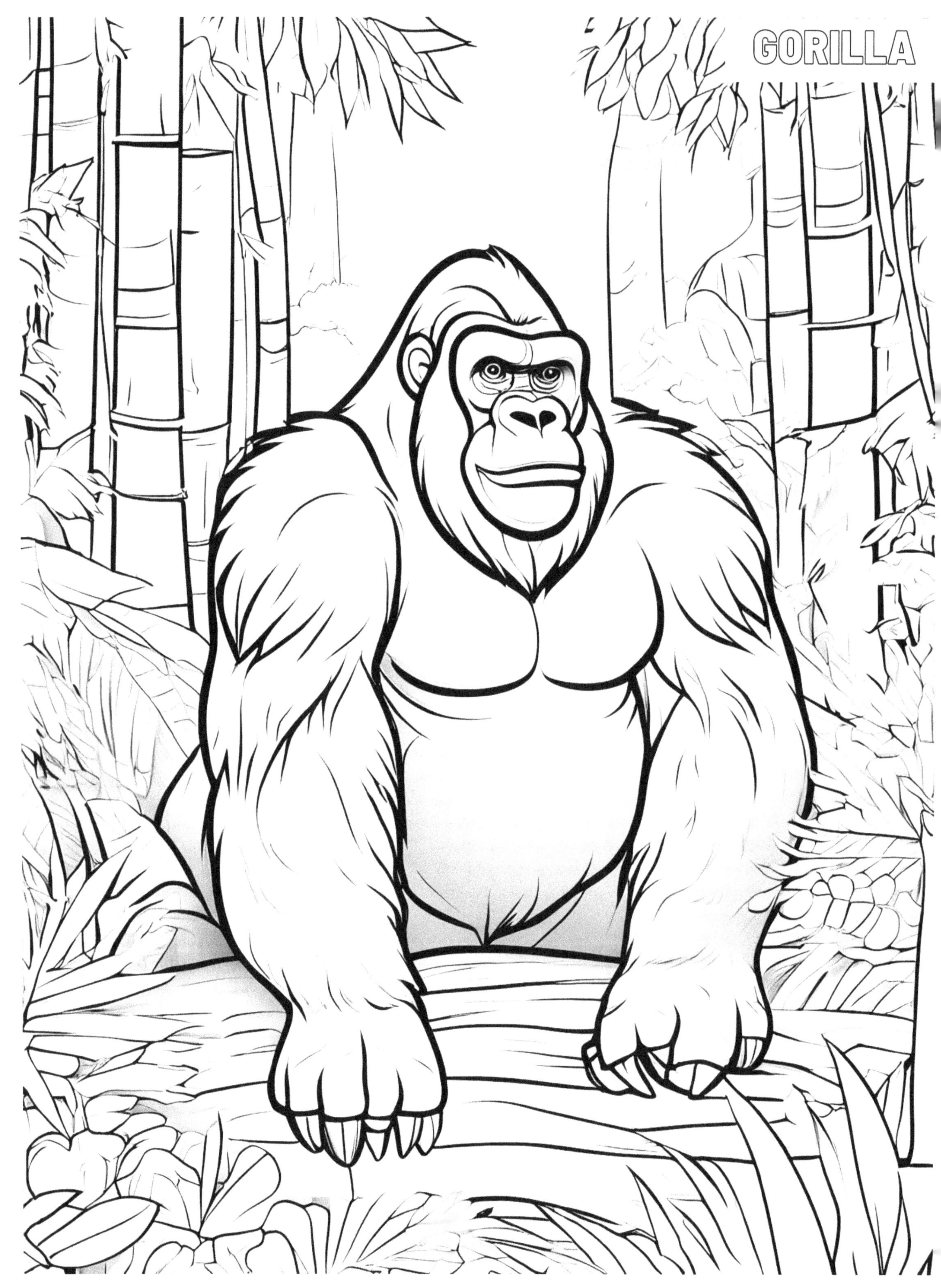
GORILLA

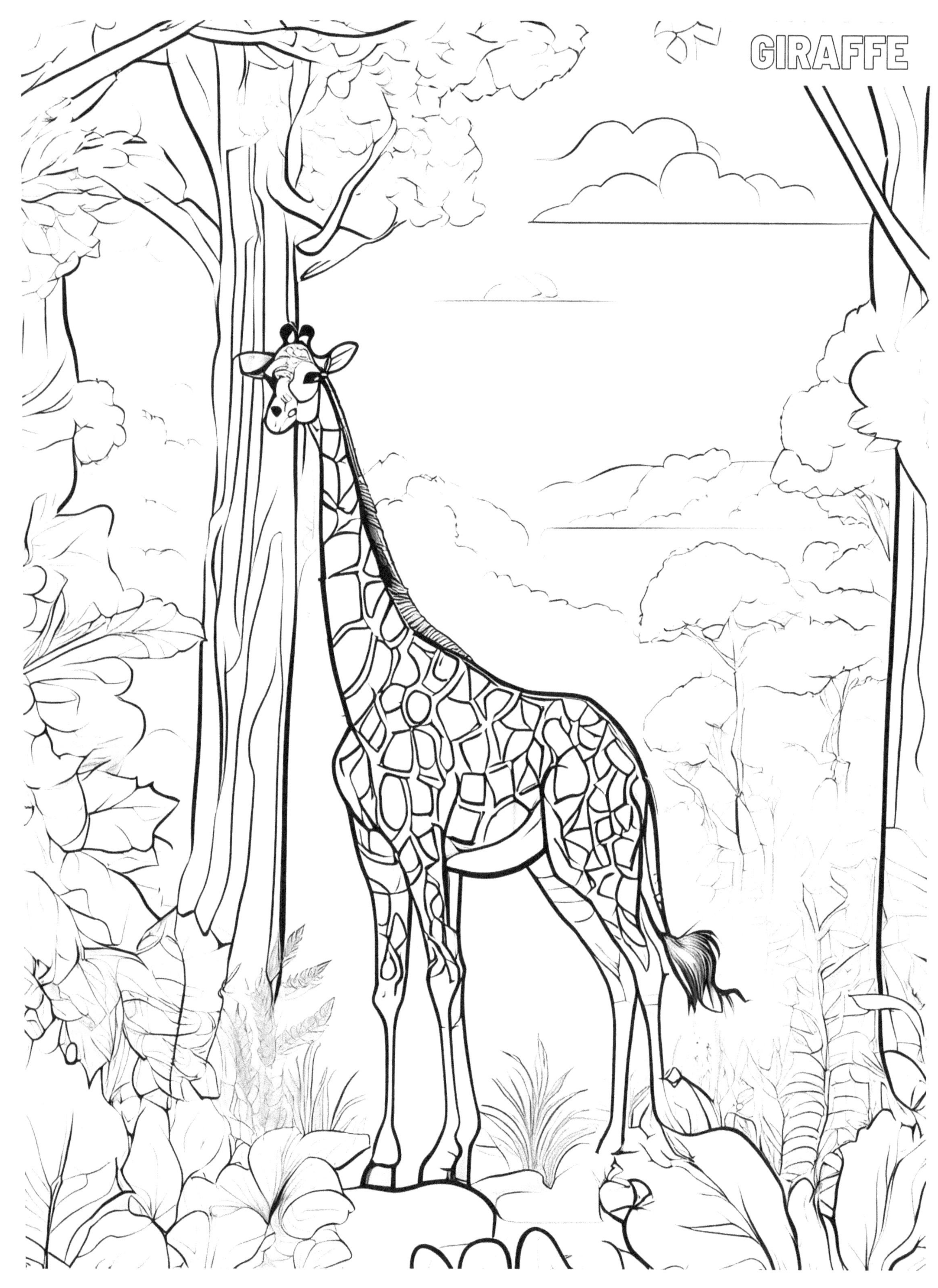

GIRAFFE

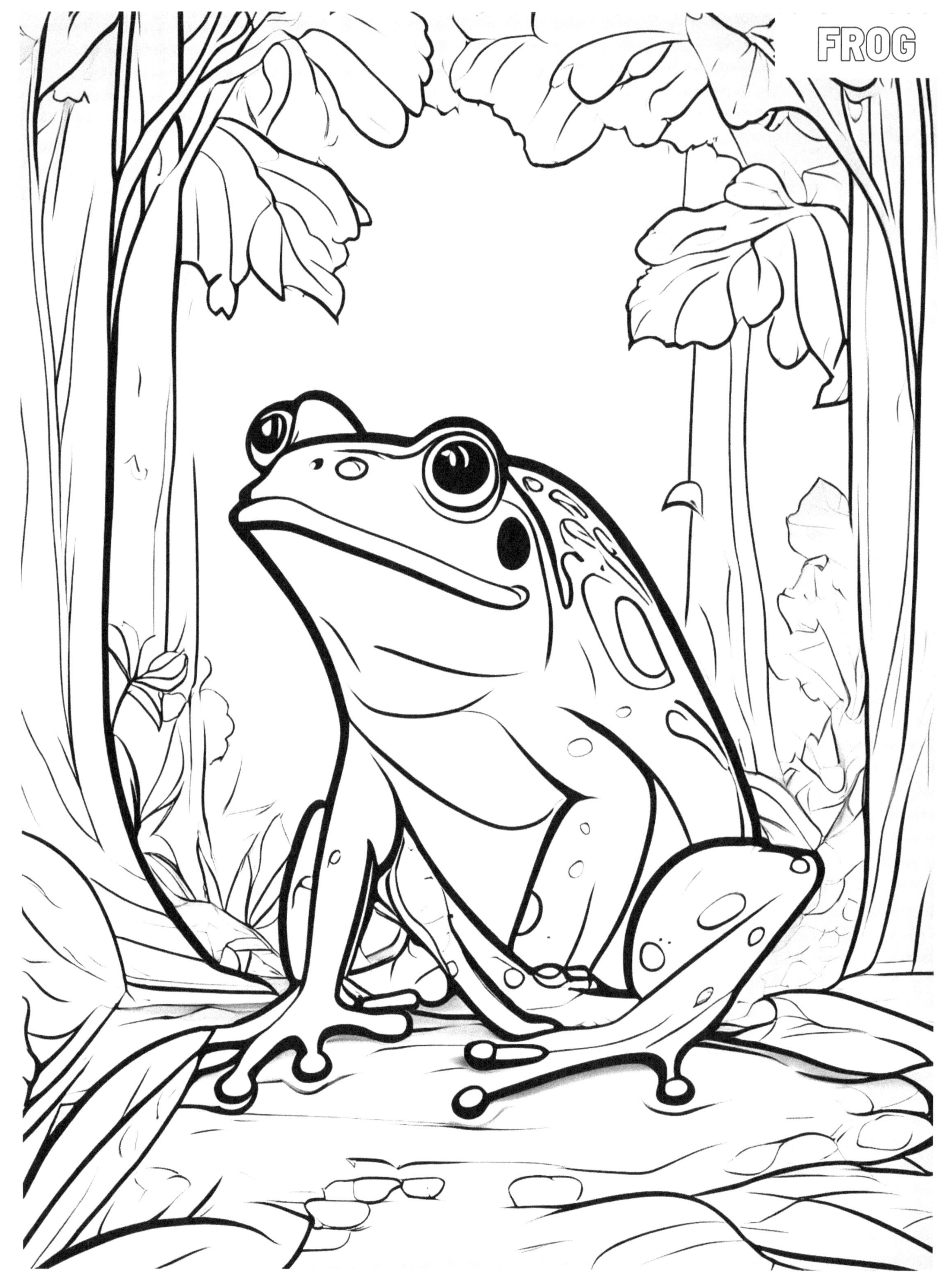
FROG

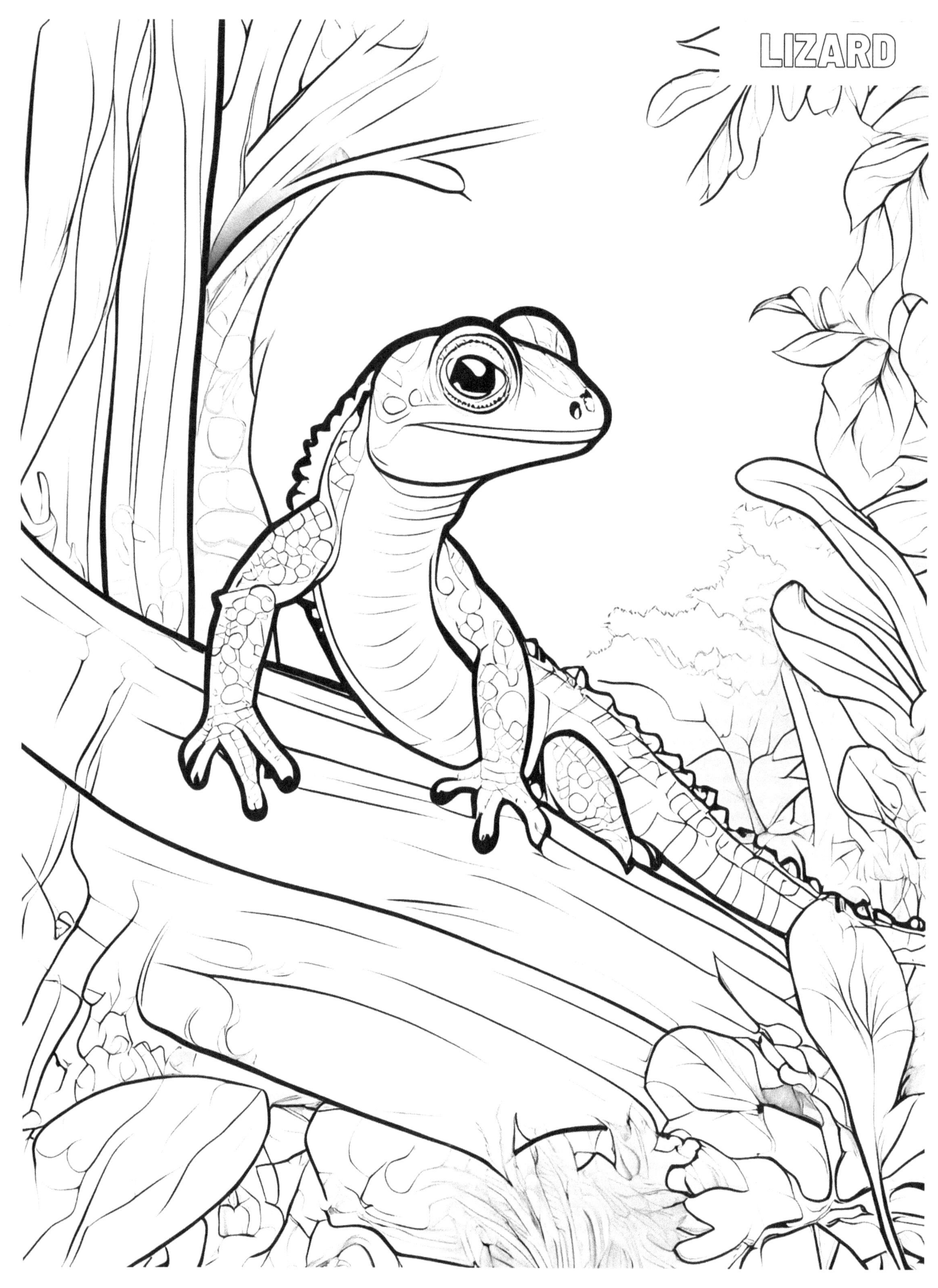

LIZARD

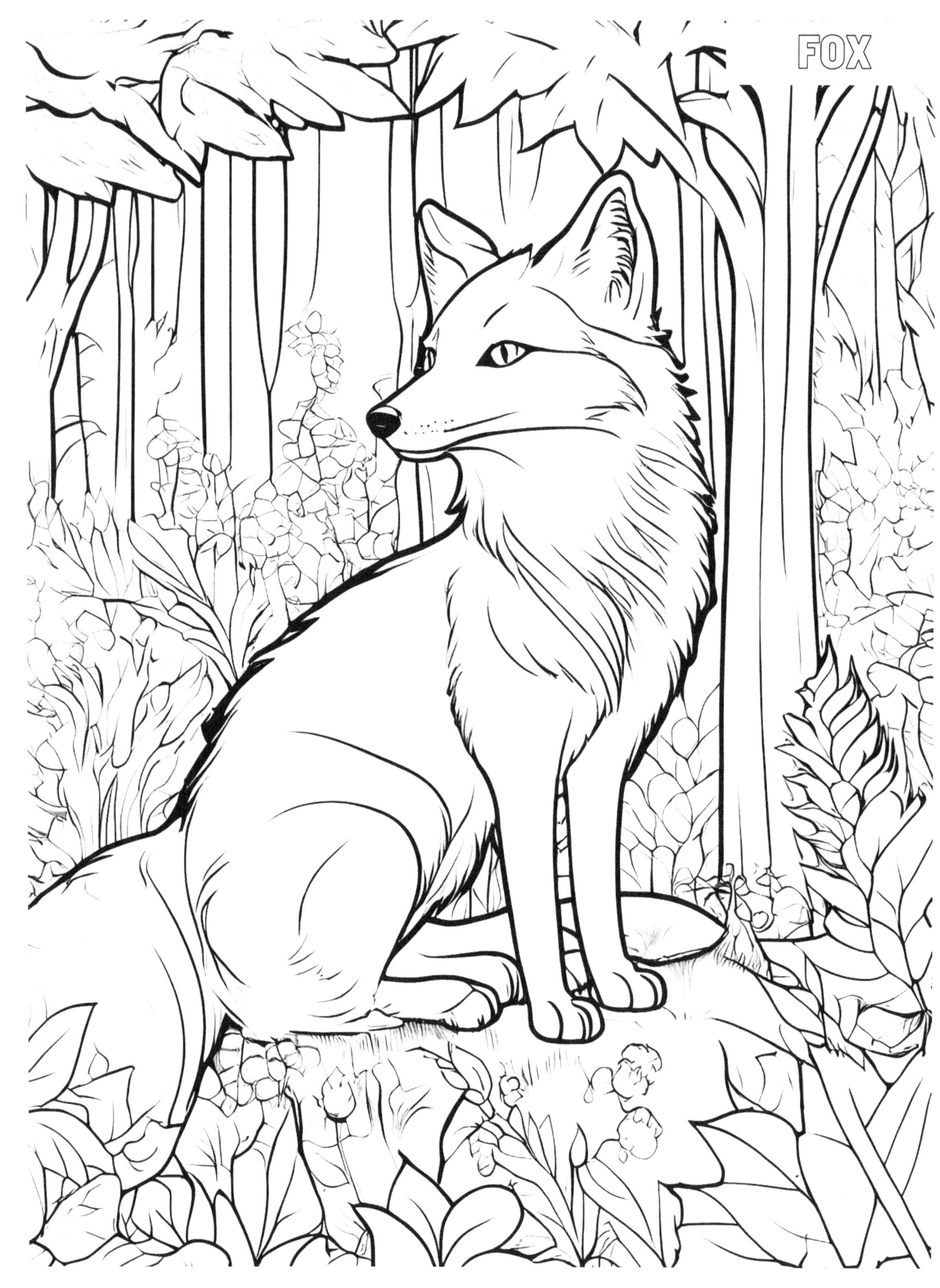
FOX

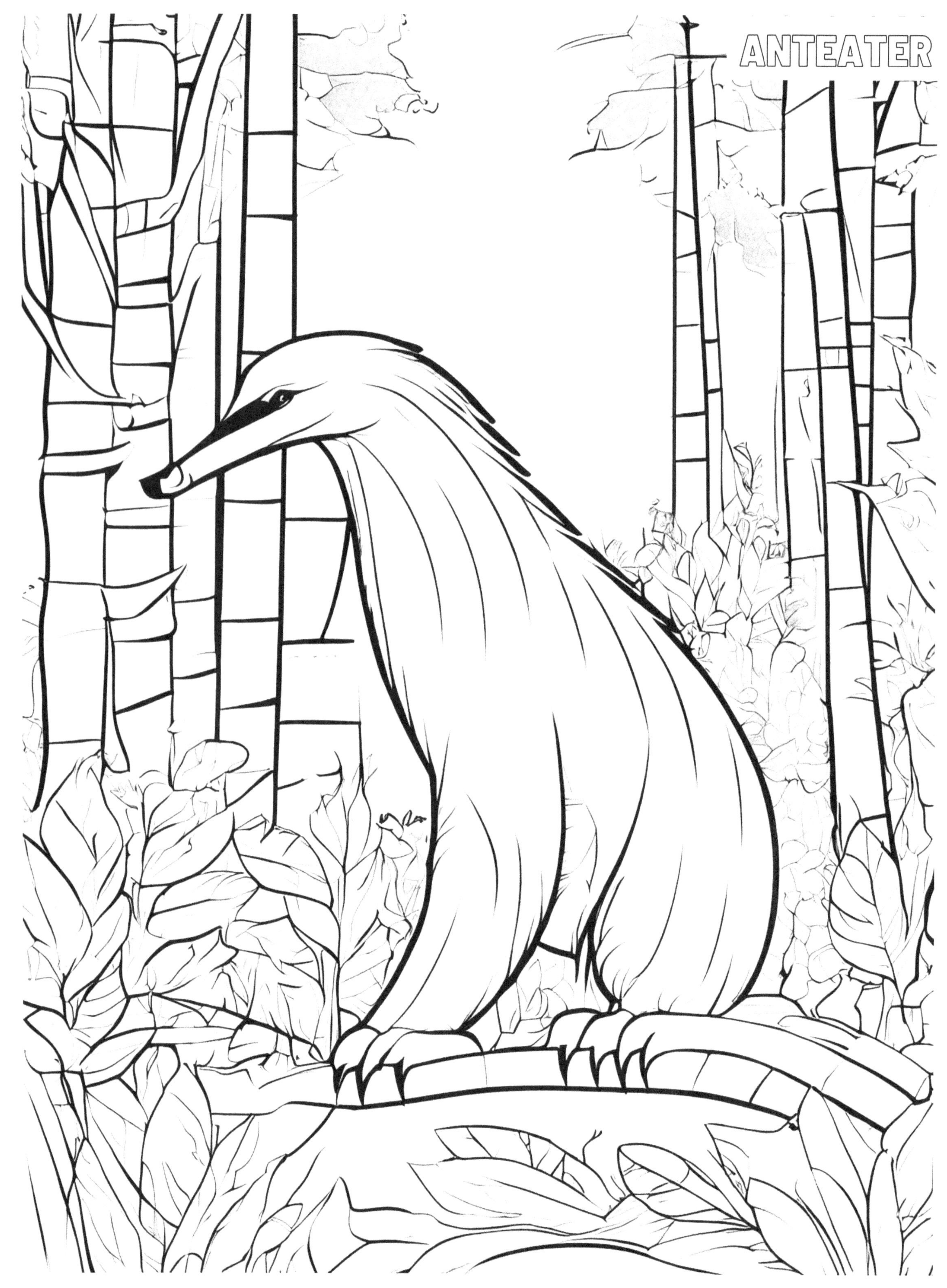

ANTEATER

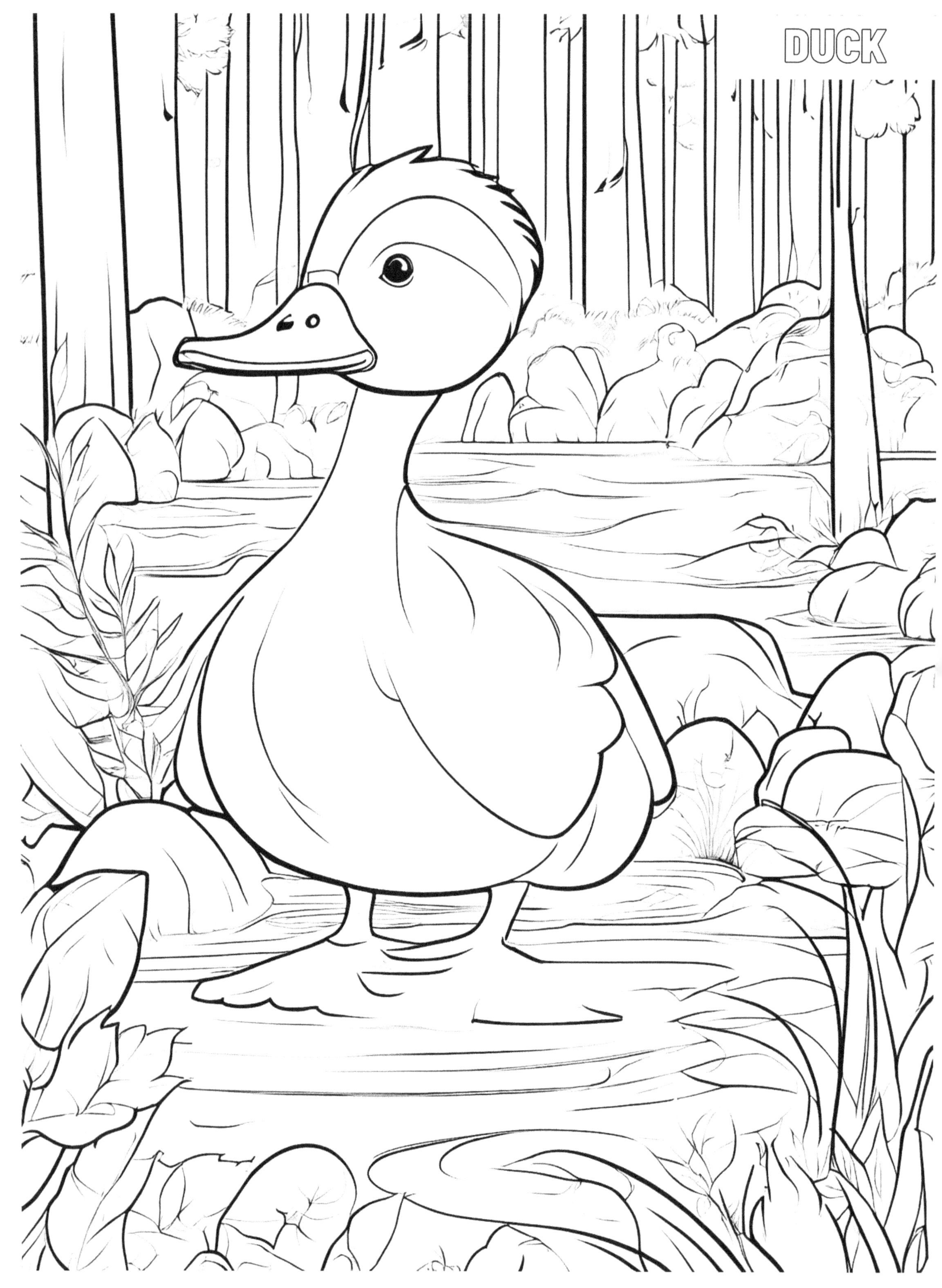

DUCK

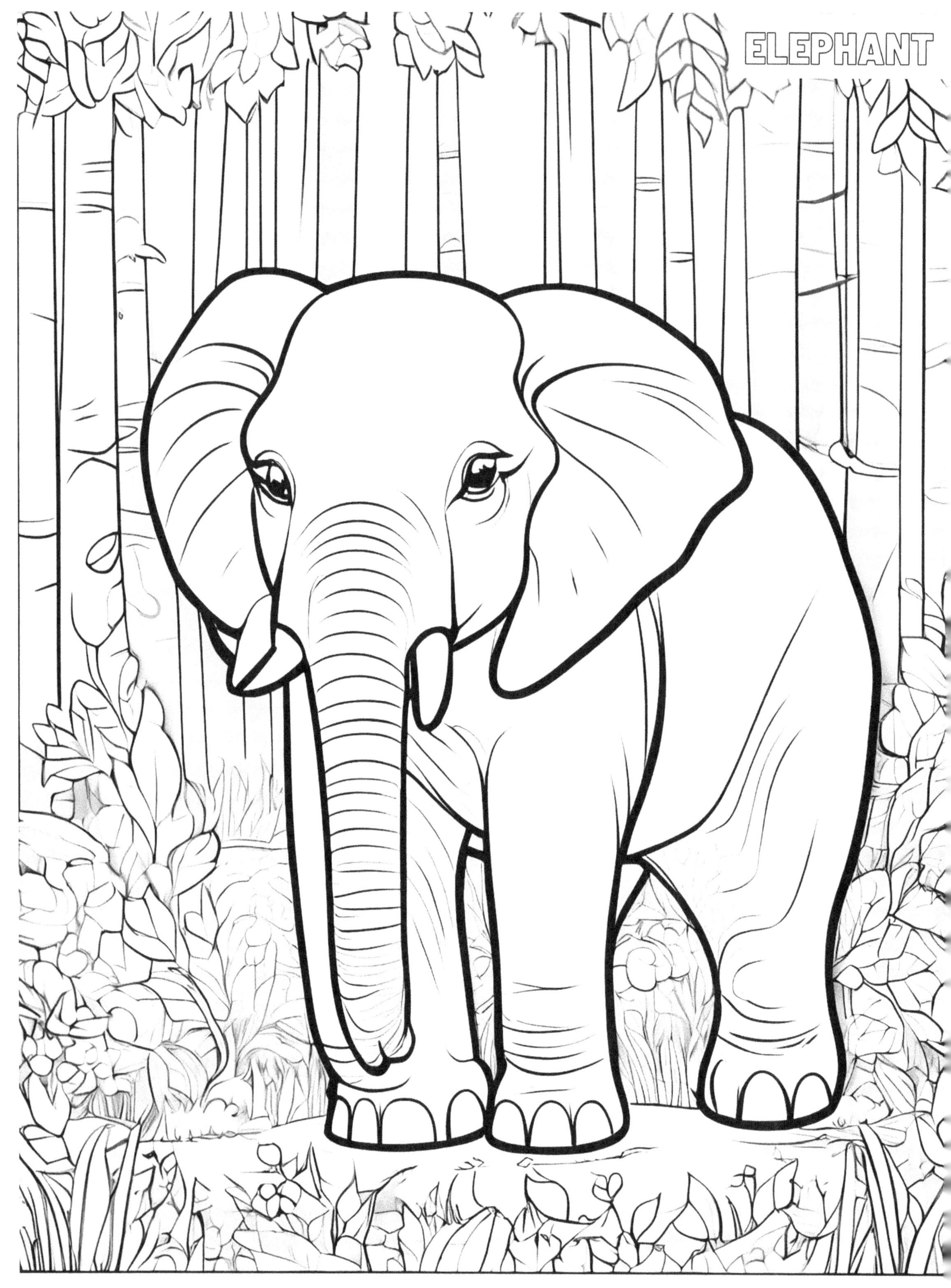

ELEPHANT

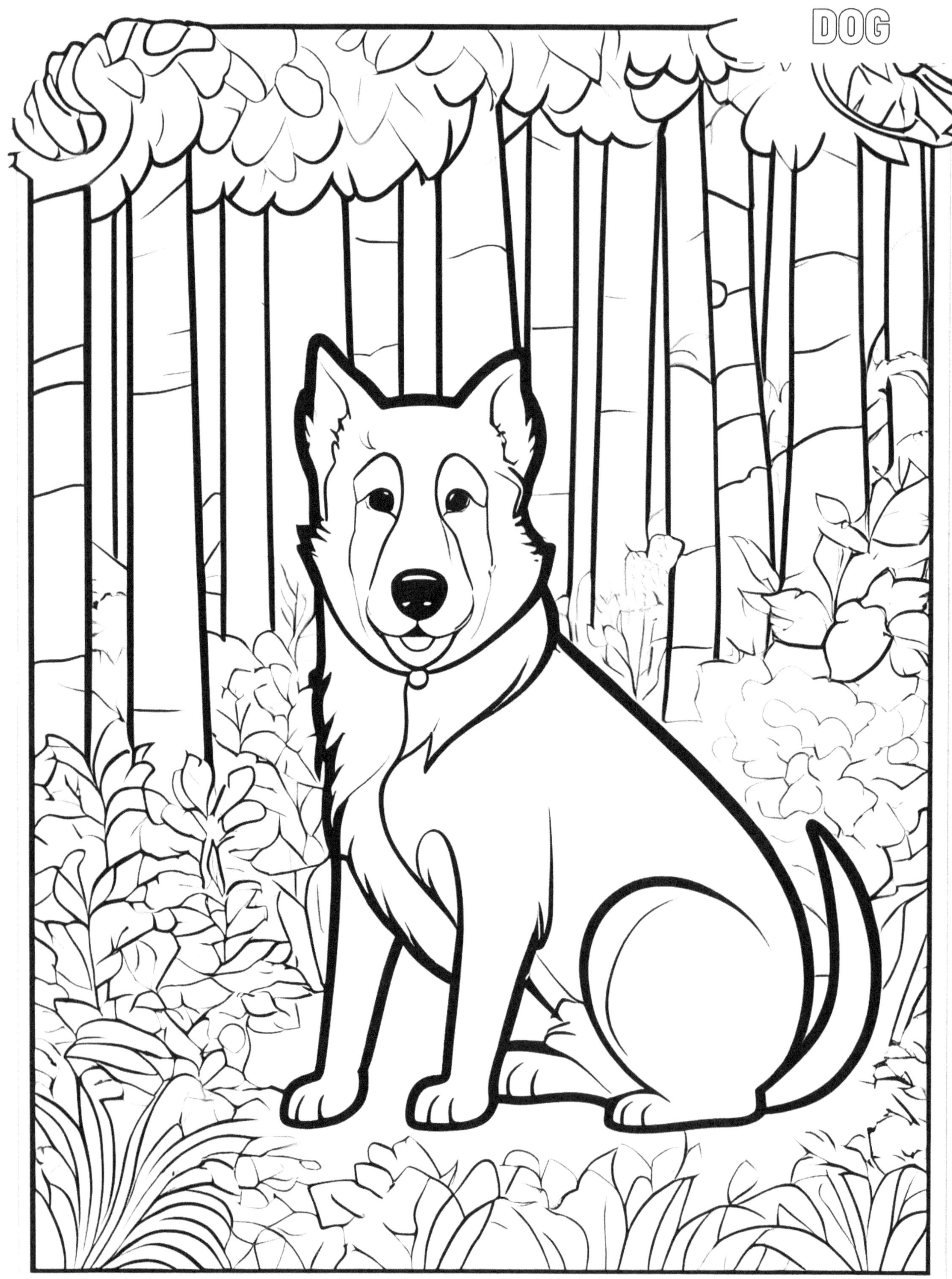
DOG

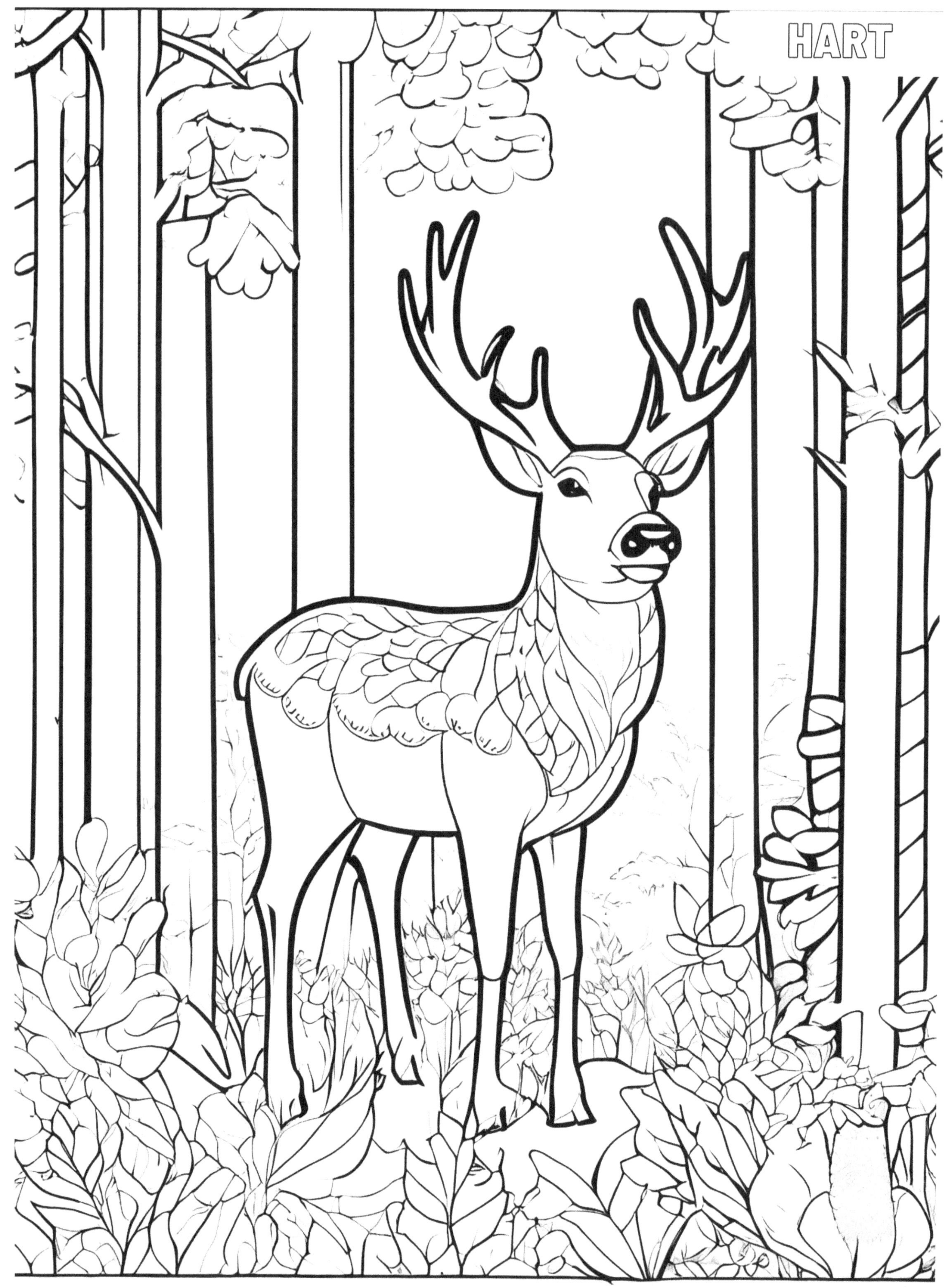

HART

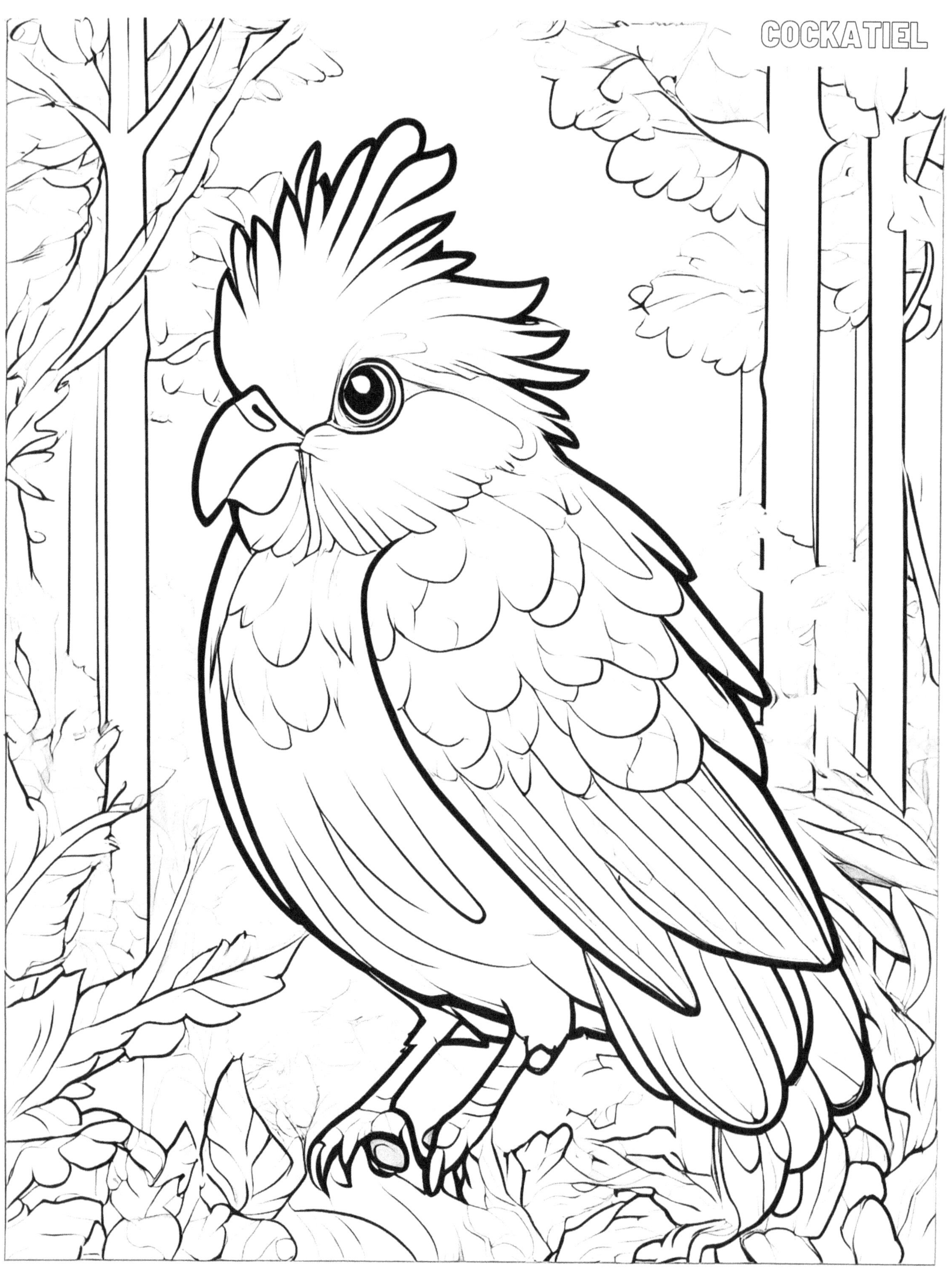
COCKATIEL

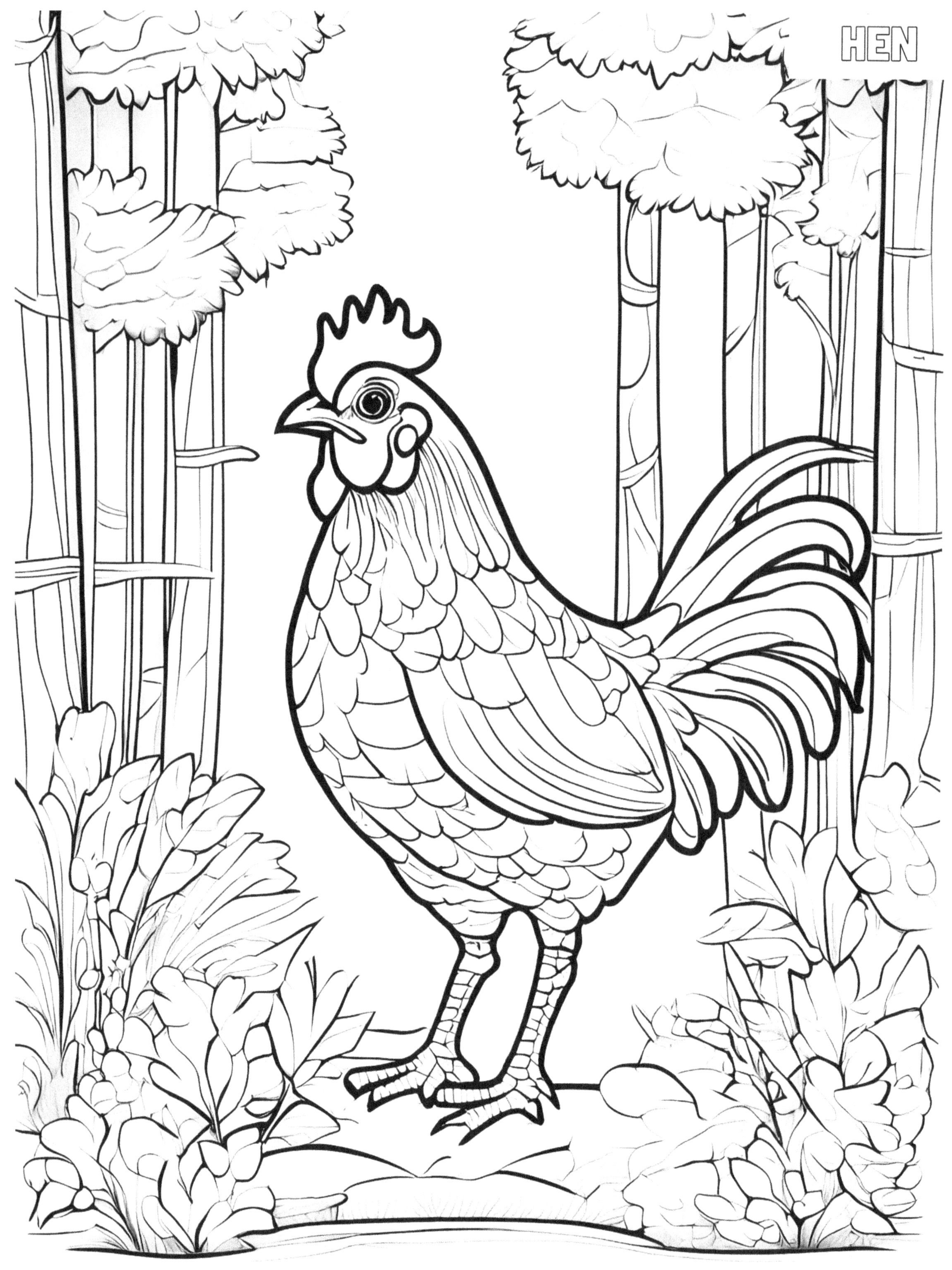

HEN

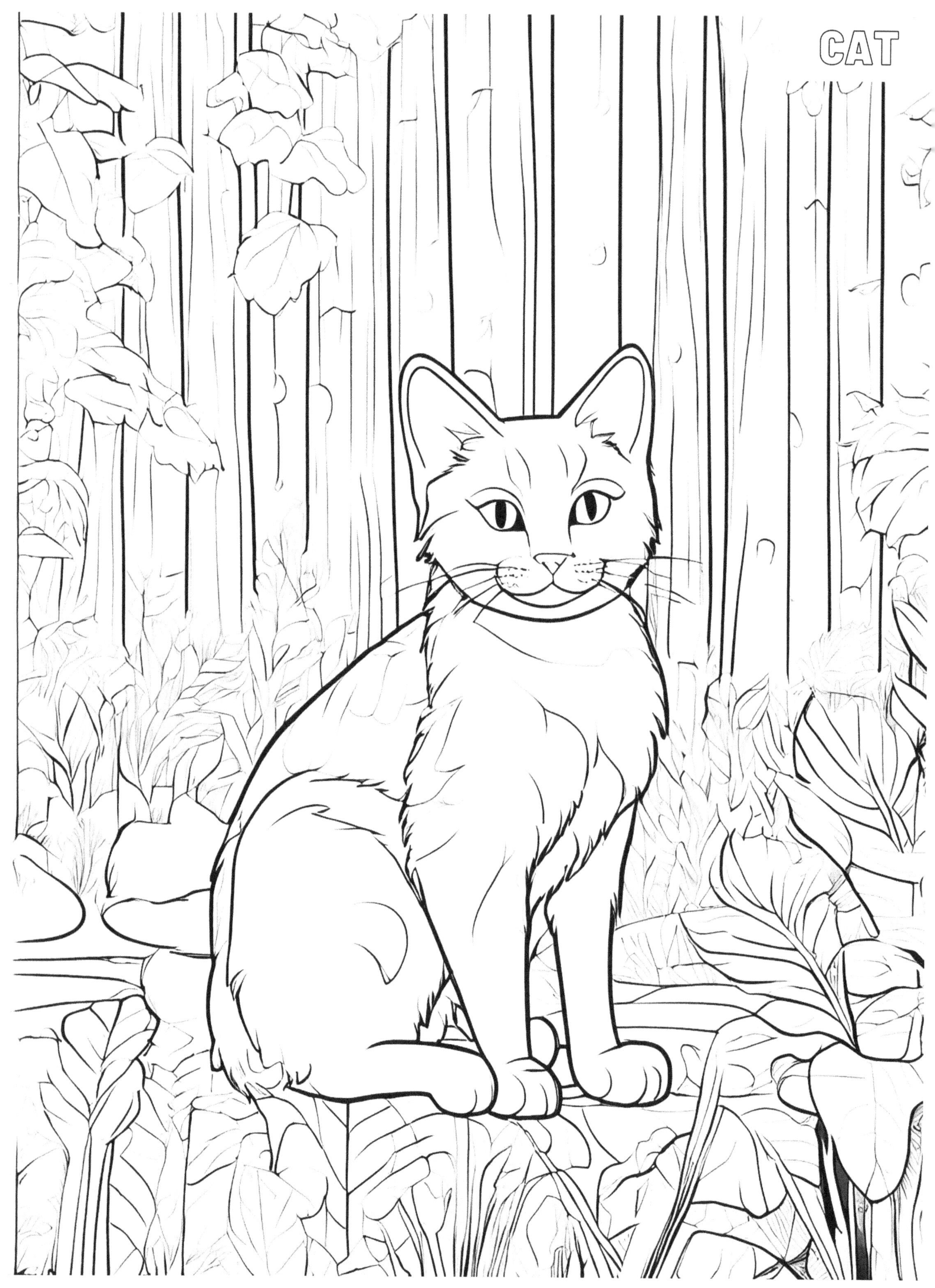
CAT

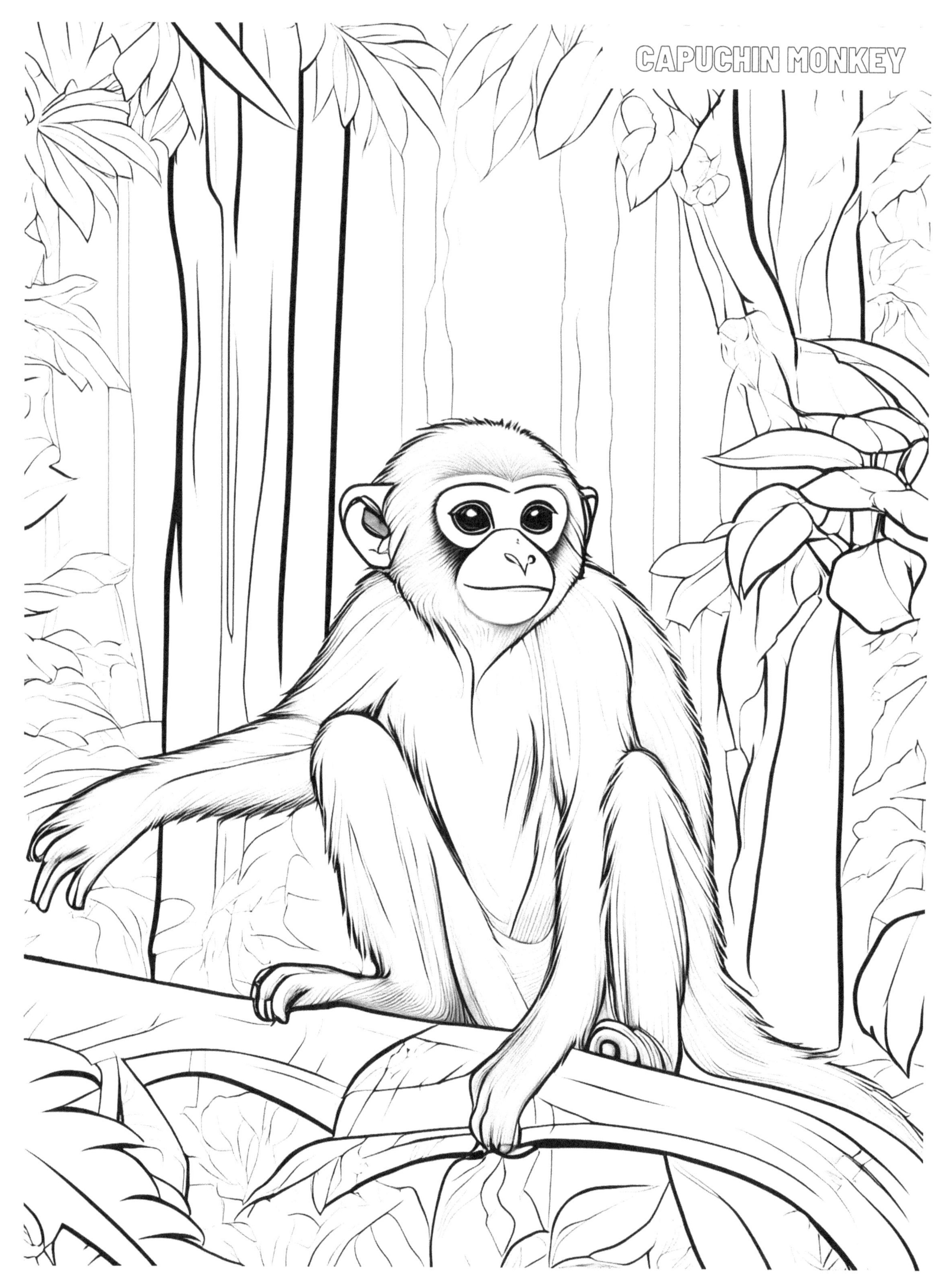
CAPUCHIN MONKEY

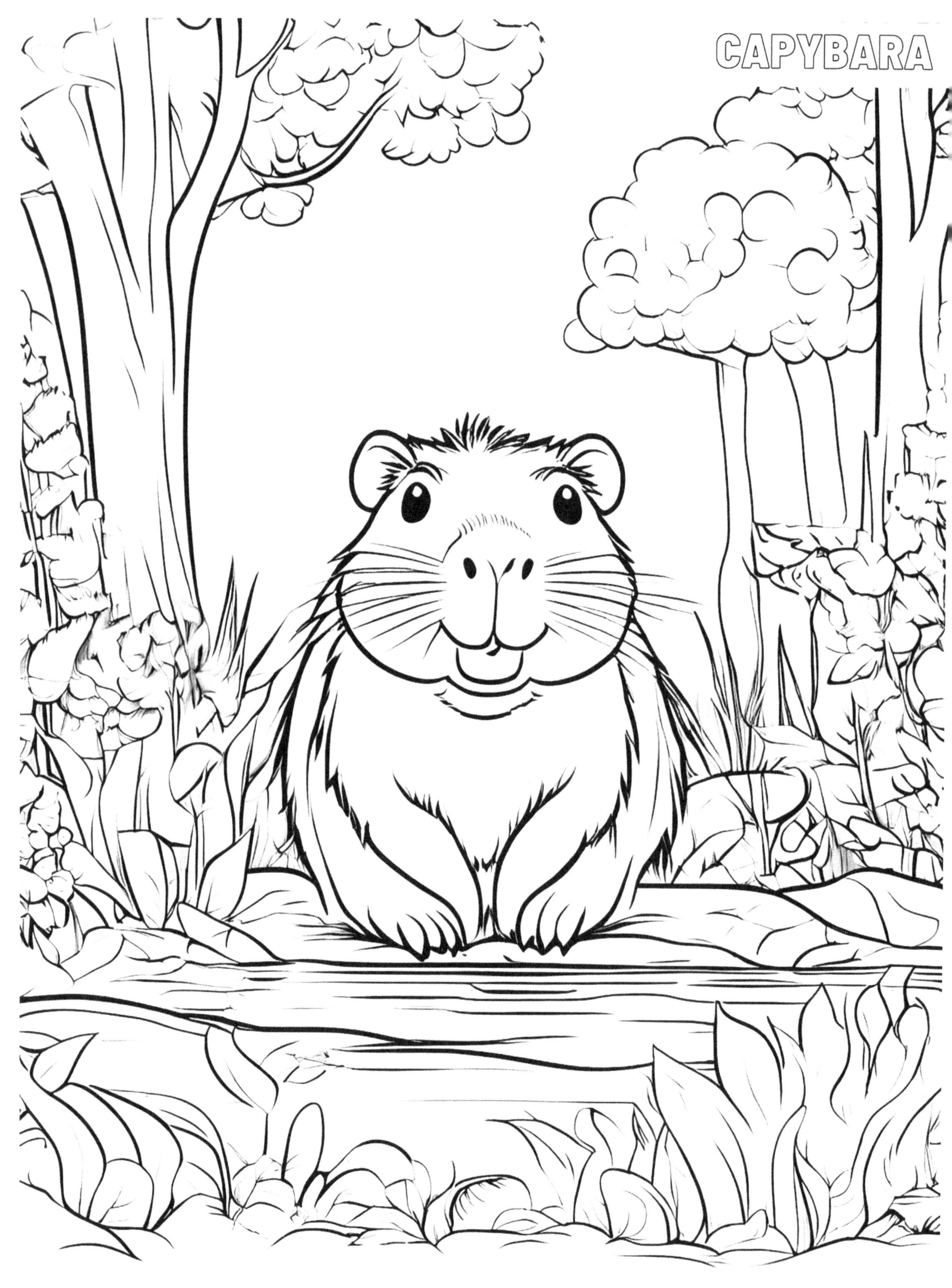

CAPYBARA

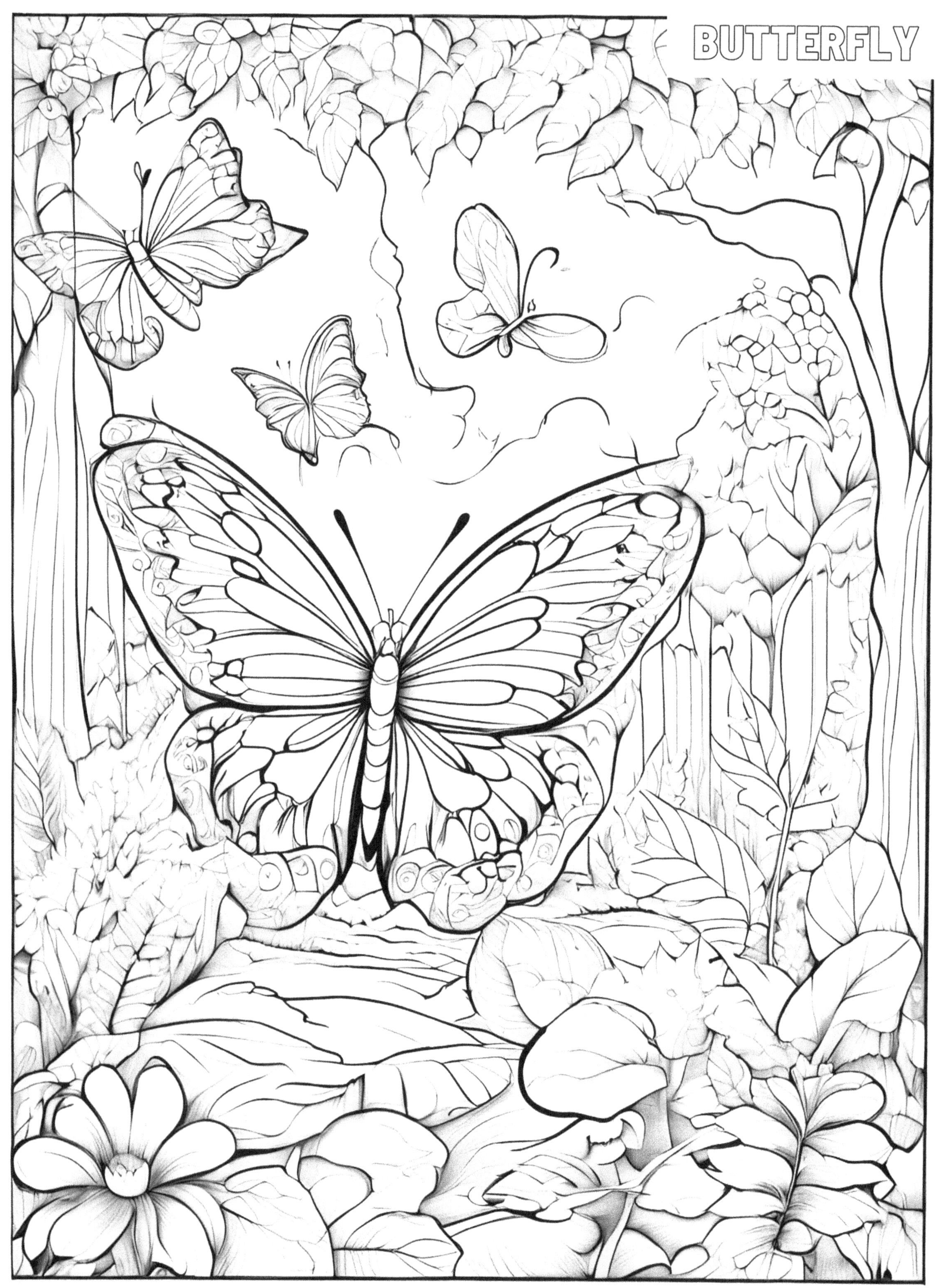
BUTTERFLY

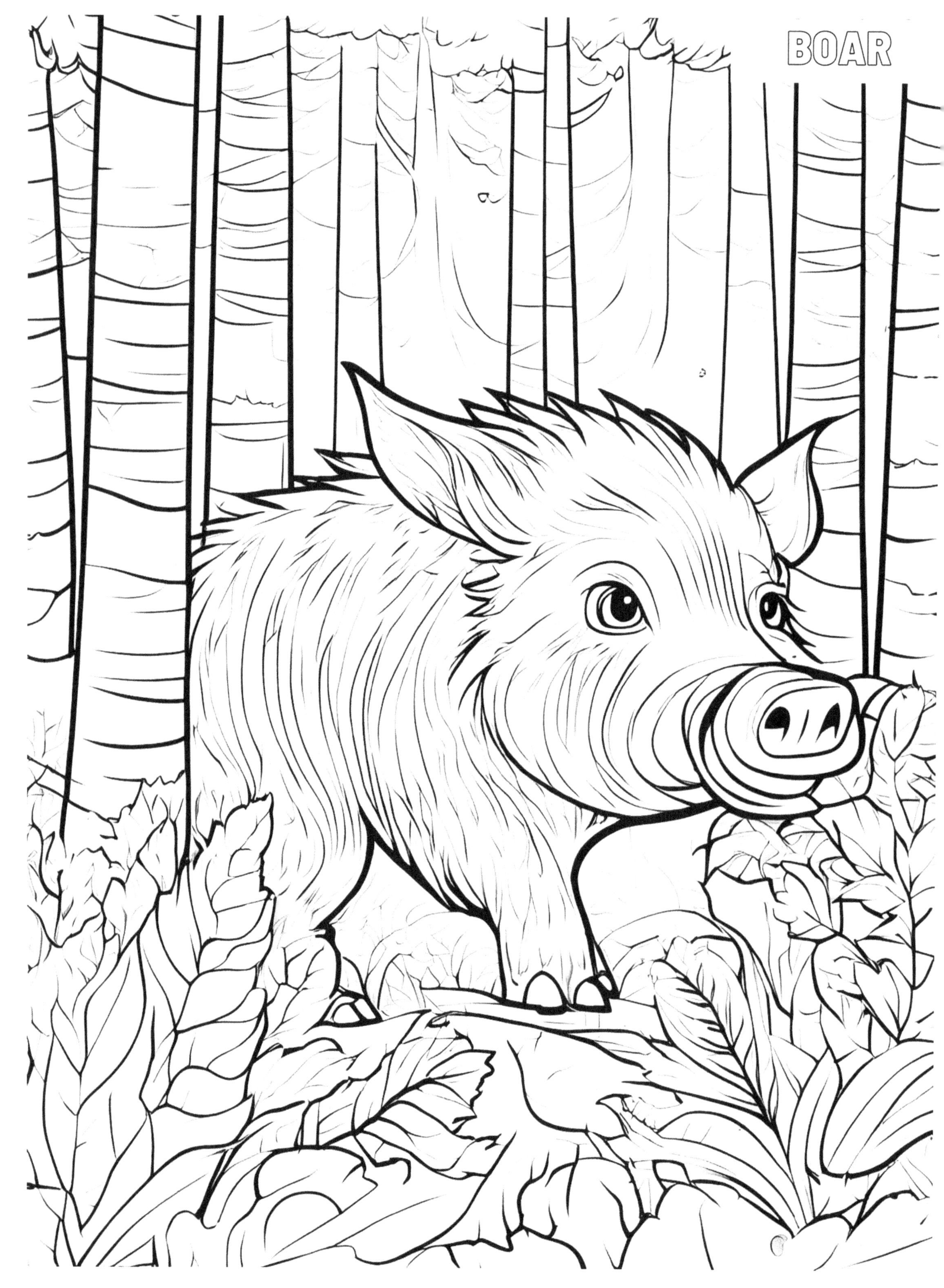
BOAR

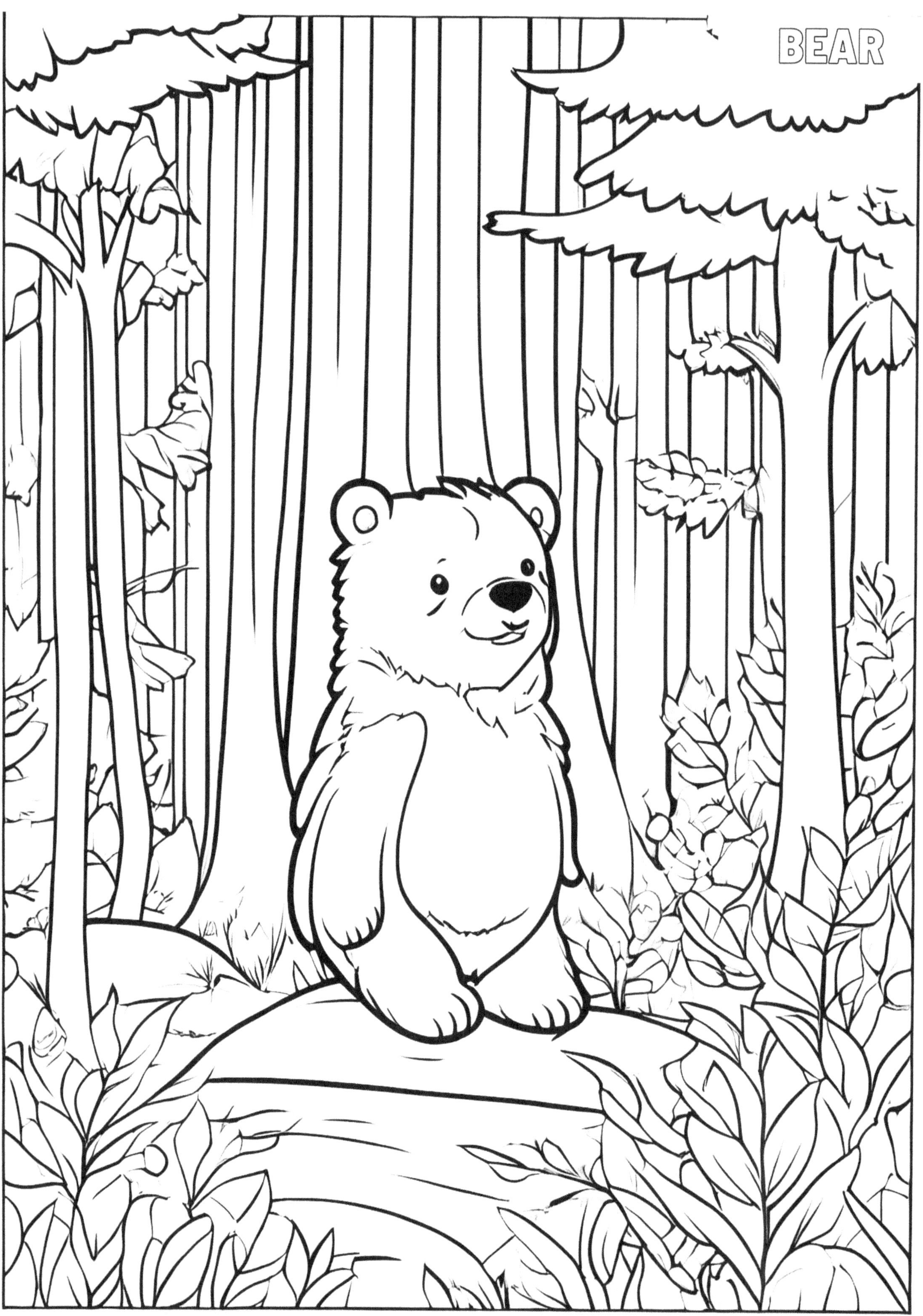
BEAR

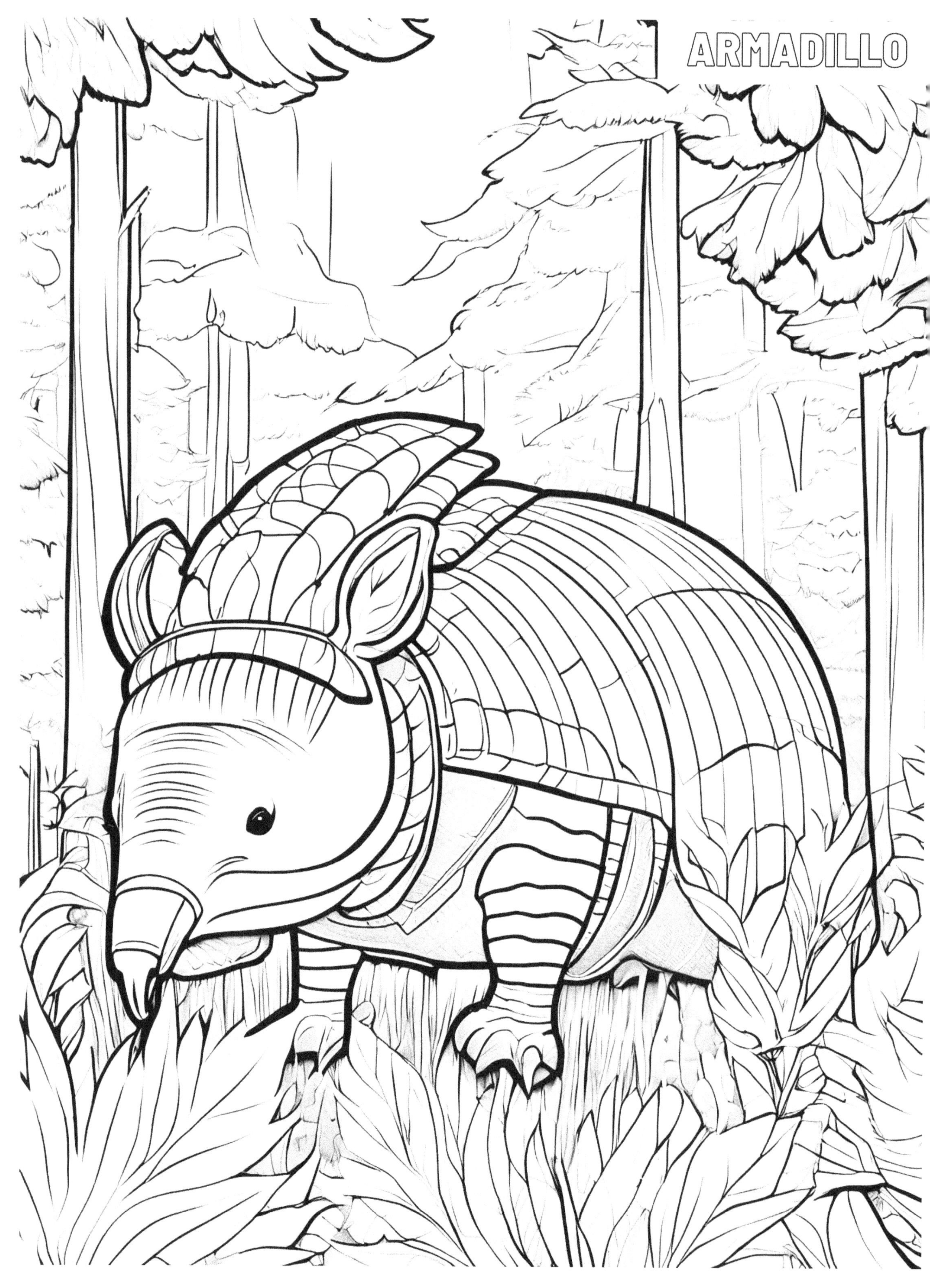
ARMADILLO

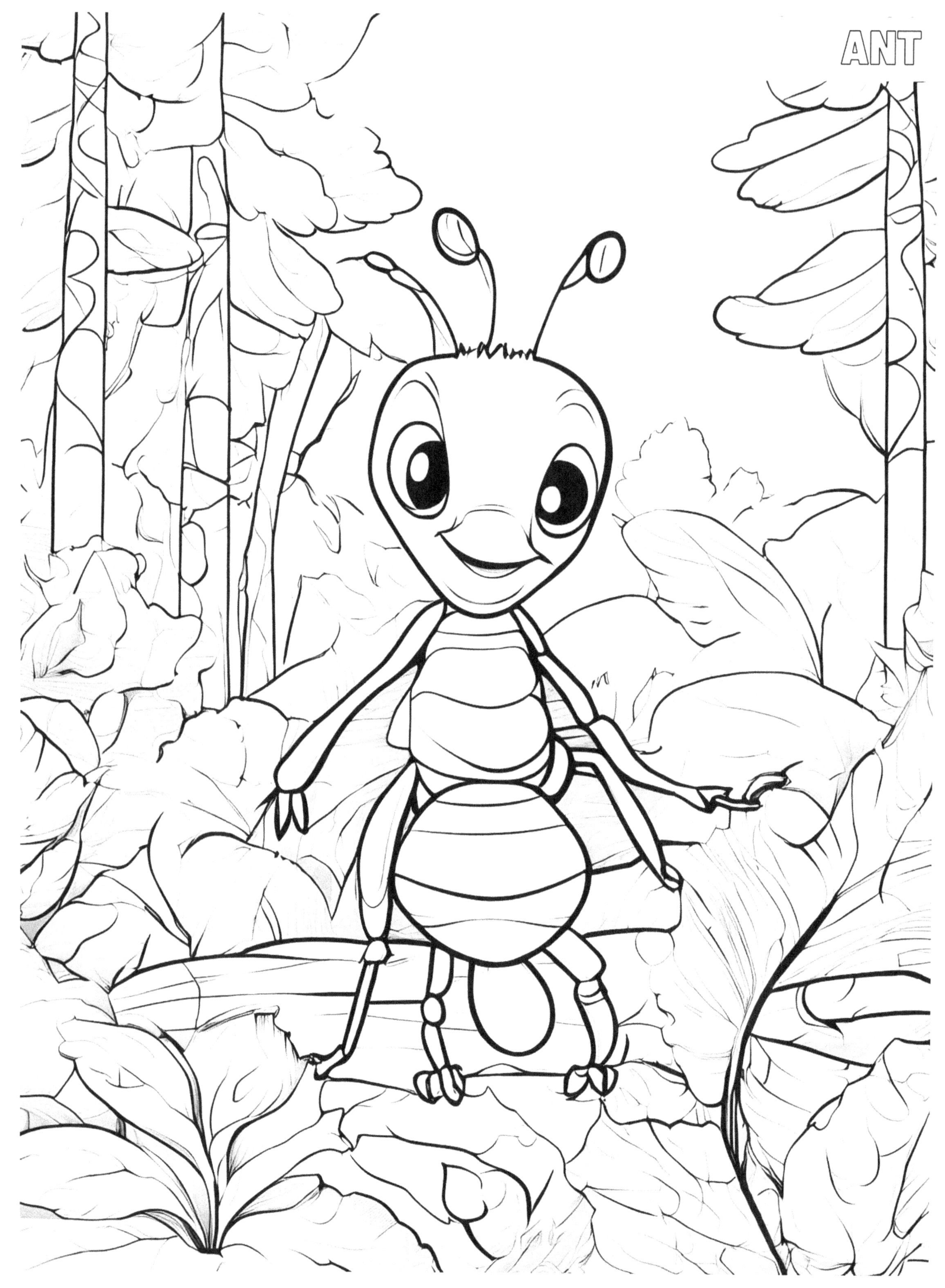
ANT

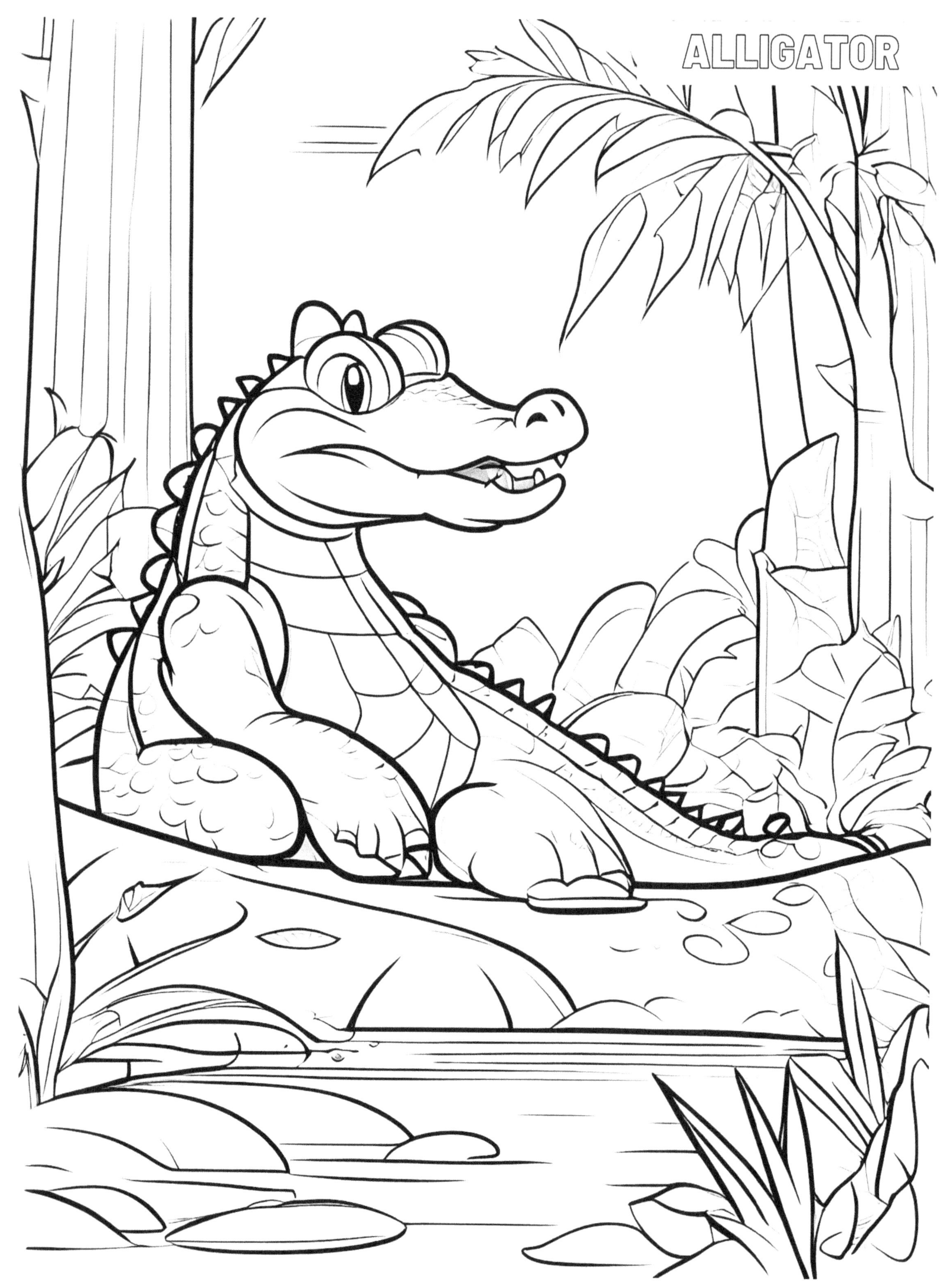

ALLIGATOR